BOOKS

THAT

SHAPED

SUCCESSFUL

PEOPLE

BOOKS

THAT

SHAPED

SUCCESSFUL

PEOPLE

EDITED BY KEVIN H. KELLY

FAIRVIEW PRESS   MINNEAPOLIS

Published by Fairview Press, 2450 Riverside Avenue South, Minneapolis, MN 55454.

Library of Congress Cataloging-in-Publication Data

Books that shaped successful people / edited by Keven H. Kelly.
    p.   cm.
    ISBN 0-925190-43-8 (cloth : alk. paper). -- ISBN 0-925190-44-6
(paper : alk. paper)
      1. Celebrities--United States--Books and reading. 2. Best books-
-United States.   I. Kelly, Kevin H., 1970-   .
  Z1039.C45B66   1995
  028 .9--dc 20   95-19441
                                      CIP

First Printing: July 1995

Printed in the United States of America
99 98 97 96 95   7 6 5 4 3 2 1

Jacket design: Circus design
Internal design: Jeffrey Kelly
Kevin Kelly's photo: Chris Rexinger

Publisher's Note: Fairview Press publishes books and other materials related to the subjects of family issues, relationships, and self help. Its publications, including *Books That Shaped Successful People* do not necessarily reflect the philosophy of Fairview Hospital and Healthcare Services or their treatment programs.

The paper used in this publication meets the minimum requirements of American National Standards for Information Sciences— Permanence of Paper for Printed Materials, ANSI Z329.48-1984.∞™

To Bubby and Grammie.

CONTENTS

ACKNOWLEDGMENTS

So many people have helped me along the way that I couldn't imagine trying to thank them all. I must however thank my friends and family for giving me the support and guidance I needed to complete this goal. Also, I would like to thank everyone at Fairview Press (especially my dedicated editor Julie) for giving me and my idea a chance to become what it is today. Finally I would like to thank my brother Jeff for taking time out of life to help make my book not only mine, but a family affair.

INTRODUCTION

This book is about reading and about the letters that I received over the last five and a half years. Each letter signifies someone, be it the actual person or assistant, who took the time to answer my question. In publishing this book I am giving you the opportunity to share in what I have been collecting via our wonderful postal system. I will not judge or comment on any of the letters individually; I feel it wouldn't do this project justice.

The letters should and do speak for themselves. They are from a wide range of people from many segments of professional work. Some chose simply to scratch down a list, while others sent up to two pages, with explanations and reasons for their selections. Each is important because they contribute to the encouragement of reading.

I started this book in 1990 while I was a sophomore at San Diego State University. At the time I was just getting back into reading again (high school seemed to be a blur of cliff notes and book-to-film movies), however the sheer number of titles intimidated me. I didn't want to just grab any book from the shelf at random. My time seemed more valuable than that. I wanted and really needed some direction.

I searched libraries and bookstores for books on reading, more specifically for reading lists by people whom I respect for their accomplishments in their fields of work. I was surprised to find no such book.

So I got the idea to write to well-known people asking them these two simple yet wordy questions: "What ten books do you feel a well-read, well-educated person should read or simply should have read? Also, what do you feel is the greatest book you have ever read?" By asking these questions I figured I could find out the information for my own needs and at the same time put together an interesting book.

I developed a form letter, which grew slightly longer as time moved on, and discovered the one truth in trying to get answers out of almost anyone: Send a self-addressed stamped envelope. Many of the people I wrote to receive hundreds, if not thousands of letters a week. Anything that makes it easier for them to respond will ensure more responses.

I chose to write to a variety of people because I wanted to represent a wide spectrum of personalities in this book. I hoped to get reading advice from as many fields as possible for I knew that this would offer the most diverse group of recommended titles. I do not necessarily endorse the views of the people found in this book.

I also realize that some of the names in this book may be unfamiliar. The short biography is meant to help you to place the individual. I define a successful person as someone whose personality or work has achieved some degree of notability in his or her particular field.

Over the course of making this book I have gotten many amusing responses relating to my letter. Probably the most exciting was when David Letterman read my letter on Friday night viewer mail.

It went like this: Letterman read my letter with the camera on my actual letter (which of course asked for a list of ten books along with his favorite), then said, "Well Kevin, I'm glad you asked." He showed a book to the camera. "This is my favorite book." The title read "How to Make Money Sending out Self-Addressed Stamped Envelopes." A definite jab at my intentions, but I like Dave and besides, how many times are you going to get the letter for your book read on national television?

Another amusing response was from the late science fiction writer Issac Assimov. He chose not to answer my question, but he did scrawl some words on the top of my original letter. He wrote "I am too old and tired to answer miscellaneous questions." This, I believe, gave me a little insight into the character of Issac Assimov (at least at the time he responded to my letter). I also got an index card from Karl Malone of the Utah Jazz. He signed the card, put his jersey number on it, and included the phrase "My favorite book." Along with this card was a catalog for Karl Malone products. I assume that this was the book he was referring to.

Also, I have easily become a member of the most fan clubs in the Western hemisphere. It got to the point where I had to put a disclaimer at the bottom of my letter to let the reader know that this was a serious endeavor so that I wouldn't automatically be placed on some list. I still receive mail from Tammy Fay Baker just about every other week.

Along with the funnier responses, I also received many disappointments along the way. After compiling all of the letters I had to rewrite each person to request permission to reproduce his or her letter. This was basically giving people an opportunity to say no. It is hard to receive a "no" after an initial "yes" but it makes me cherish the people that did go out of their way to say yes twice.

To be expected, some of the people that initially responded have since passed away. The inclusion of their letters is important because it helps their legacy live on through written words. One touching letter that I received was from the wife of late writer Howard Lemerov. She said that she was more than grateful to have me reproduce his list of books because they were written a few weeks before his death, which he knew was imminent.

I can honestly say that this book that I have put together has influenced me. I definitely have chosen to read specific books because of recommendations. I chose *The Basketball Diaries* by Jim Carroll because Woody Harrelson had it on his list. I read *The Idiot* by Dostoyevski because of Allen Ginsberg and *Magic Mountain* by Thomas Mann because Michael Manley, the Prime Minister of Jamaica, spoke highly of it. I know that these letters will continue to affect me because I will turn to it to choose other books to read throughout my life.

What we read influences and shapes us daily. If we are products of everything around us and everything we've done up until now, then everything we read shapes our thinking in some way. The recommendations in this book can help you to navigate the vast sea of books with some confidence that others have sailed these waters before you.

For entertainment and curiosity's sake I tallied up every response chosen so that I could make a list of the top fifteen responses chosen over-all. Here's the list:

1. *The Bible*
2. *Huckleberry Finn* by Mark Twain
3. Works of William Shakespeare
4. *Hamlet* by William Shakespeare

5. *War and Peace* by Leo Tolstoy
6. *The Iliad* by Homer
7. *The Odyssey* by Homer
8. *The Catcher in the Rye* by J. D. Salinger
9. *The Sound and the Fury* by William Faulkner
10. *The Prophet* by Kahlil Gibran
11. *The Brothers Karamazov* by Fyodor Dostoyevski
12. *Gone with the Wind* by Margaret Mitchell
13. *The Grapes of Wrath* by John Steinbeck
14. *A Tale of Two Cities* by Charles Dickens
15. *The Inferno* by Dante

As the project progressed I found that a great deal of books that I was supposed to read in high school were the ones that most people recommended. It appears that the canon of Western literature still has influence over the majority of the respondents. I came to realize that these selections could be either what these people really read or what they want to be perceived as having read. You will have to judge for yourself as you wander through the following pages.

Enough of my rambling. This book is really about the letters and reading suggestions of knowledgeable and successful people. Let me simply be your guide as you read my mail. I hope you enjoy this as much as I have enjoyed working on it.

"Books are the treasure wealth of the world and the fit inheritance of generations and nations."

Henry David Thoreau, *Walden*

Reading is one of the great pleasures of my life.
Literally anything is possible once you learn to
read. Information, adventure, romance, suspense,
wisdom, lunacy, all things are available on the
printed page.

Best always,

John Landis

ENTERTAINERS

John Landis

Director

Film credits include *Coming to America, An American Werewolf in London, Animal House,* and Michael Jackson's "Thriller" video.

MCA INC., 100 UNIVERSAL CITY PLAZA, UNIVERSAL CITY, CALIFORNIA 91608

Writer's Direct Dial

(818) 777-

June 3, 1991

Dear Kevin:

    I have been a voracious reader since I was a little boy, so trying to make any sort of "list of 10 books that influenced me" would be a fruitless task. There are just too many great books.

    I find any sort of "ten best list" impossible in books or film. For example, how does one compare Disney's PINOCCHIO (a great film) with Hitchcock's PSYCHO (another great film)?

    I am a tremendous admirer of Mark Twain, Philip Roth, E.B. White, Isaac Bashevis Singer, Graham Greene, Vladimir Nabokov, Evelyn Waugh, T.H. White, Saul Bellow, A.A. Milne, Charles Dickens, William Boyd, P.G. Wodhouse, George Bernard Shaw, and Larry McMurtry. All of these are just names off the top of my head. With deeper thought, I'm sure I'd come up with many, many more.

    I really don't mean to sound facile, it's just that I read a lot, and not just fiction. I am also a fan of autobiography, biography and history books.

Mr. Kevin H. Kelly
June 3, 1991
Page 2

    Certainly not the "greatest book" I ever read, but perhaps my favorite, is Mark Twain's <u>A Connecticut Yankee in King Arthur's Court</u>. It is deeply flawed but the originality and passion with which it is written is very exciting to me.

    Good luck with your project.

               Sincerely,

               John Landis

JL/sd

August 15, 1991

Kevin H. Kelly
5584 Hardy Ave. #101
San Diego, CA 92115

Dear Mr. Kelly:

As you requested, below is the list (in no particular order)
of the ten books that have most influenced Woody Harrelson.

Heart of Darkness, Joseph Conrad

The Fountainhead, Ayn Rand

The Sound and the Fury, William Faulkner

Think on these Things, Krishnamurti

Lolita, Vladimir Nabakov

The Basketball Diaries, Jim Carroll

The Return of the Bird Tribes, Ken Carey

The Adventures of Huckleberry Finn, Mark Twain

A People's History of the United States, Howard Zinn

We hope this will help you in your research. Woody wanted to
pass along his appreciation for asking the question-- it
required him to sit down and think quietly for a few minutes,
something which he rarely has an opportunity to do while at
work.

Good luck with your book, and take care.

Sincerely,

Kelly Ferguson
Asst. to Woody Harrelson

Woody Harrelson

Actor/Entertainer

Starred in the *Cheers* television series. Film credits include
White Men Can't Jump and *Natural Born Killers*.

Robin Leach

Entertainer

Host of television's *Lifestyles of the Rich and Famous.*

The Holy Bible
Days of Grace — Arthur Ashe
Homer's The Iliad
Murdoch — William Shawcross

James Bond — Ian Fleming
Raise The Titanic
Rogets Thesaurus
Funk + Wagnells New Intl. Dictionary

3-Pack of: - Art of Living
- Champagne + Caviar
- The Cigar Companion

The History Of Television

Dear Mr. Leach,

I am an English major at San Diego State University currently working on a book about what knowledgeable and successful people read. I understand that your time is valuable, so I'll make this brief. I would like nothing more than a list of ten books that you feel a well read and well educated person should read or simply should have read. Also, I would like to know what you feel is the greatest book you have ever read(it doesn't have to be on your initial list). I have compiled a group of over one hundred responses from people like Allen Ginsberg, Jane Goodall, and David Letterman, but without your input I feel it would be entirely incomplete(I am presently negotiating with a publisher, so time is somewhat of the essence). I would greatly appreciate any response(even a quick note on this letter itself). I believe reading is terribly important and I fear that children are opting to get their information visually rather than through reading. Thank you for your time and have a nice forever.

← The Gnole by Alan Aldridge

good luck

Sincerely,

Kevin H. Kelly

P.S. This is a serious endeavor, so please don't just send me fan mail information. Thank you again.

Larry King

Entertainer

Host of the *Larry King Show* television program.

May 16, 1911

Dear Kevin:

Thank you for writing the Larry King Show.

Larry's favorite books; all baseball books,
author David Halberstam books, mystery writer
Dick Francis books and currently, Lou Cannon book on
"The Reagans."

His all time favorite book is "Catcher in the Rye."

Sincerely,

Judith Thomas
Associate Producer
LKS

Mutual Broadcasting System, 1755 South Jefferson Davis Highway, Arlington, Virginia 22202

Jeff Foxworthy

Comedian/Entertainer

Stand-up comedian. Author of *You Might be a Redneck if...*

Dear Kevin

Thanks so much for including me in this project. Anything that stresses the importance of reading is indeed a noble goal. I myself am a voracious reader. I read several books a week on a variety of subjects. I also read at least one newspaper a day as well as magazines and cereal boxes!

My Grandmother taught me the love of books, at an early age. I found them to be not only a source of learning but a magic way to escape using your own imagination.

As a comedian I try to do the same thing. To get people to create a mental image through the use of words. Words are perhaps the most powerful tool man has ever invented

As for ten books that everyone should read, that is very tough. Here is a poke at it

① YOU MIGHT BE A REDNECK IF....
    (SORRY, BUT MY BABIES NEED NEW SHOES!)
② THE BIBLE
③ ILLUSIONS BY RICHARD BACH
④ CATCHER IN THE RYE
⑤ WENDAL, HIS CAT, AND THE PROGRESS OF MAN BY CAMPUDONI
⑥ MODERN MANNERS BY P.J O'ROURKE
⑦ THE DEER SLAYER
⑧ THE GREAT GATSBY
⑨ OH! THE PLACES YOU WILL GO! BY DR. SUESS
⑩ LOVE YOU FOREVER BY MUNSCH

It's just a start!
Keep Reading
Best Wishes

Jeff Foxworthy

Dear Kevin:

Sorry it took so long for me to write back. I've been real busy but I just wanted to send a quick "thank you" for your letter and send you the list you requested.

Unfortunately, I don't have much time to think it over, so these are just the first ten books that came to mind. I'm sure I'm leaving many other influential books out. I would say the first one on the list would be by favorite:

> SLAUGHTERHOUSE FIVE by Kurt Vonnegut
> BREAKFAST OF CHAMPIONS by Kurt Vonnegut
> ROOKIE AT LEAF CAMP by Scott Young
> WHEN THE SHOOTING STOP by Ralph Rosenbloom
> SIRENS OF TITAN by Kurt Vonnegut
> SIDHARTHA by Herman Hesse
> WITHOUT FEATHERS by Woody Allen
> SLAPSTICK by Kurt Vonnegut
> CURIOUS GEORGE by H.A. Rey
> P.S. I LOVE YOU by Michael Sellers

Looking over this list, I guess you could say I like Kurt Vonnegut. I hope this helps.

Good luck and party on.

Sincerely,

Mike Myers

PS I've thought about Joseph Campbell's "Hero With A Thousand Faces" is my all time favourite.

Mike Myers

Comedian/Entertainer

Starred in the *Saturday Night Live* television series.
Film credits include *Wayne's World*, *Wayne's World II*, and
So I Married an Axe Murderer.

Joan Baez

Musician/Entertainer

Album titles include *Any Day Now*, *Ballad Book*, and *Baptism*.

Joan Chandos Baez

2/7/91

Dear Kevin:

I'm sure Joan has read Ten books — + En-joyed some, but she's not here now to tell me which they are. She's not an all-time reader, but I do remember that her first + most loved book was Dickens' Autobiography — + I can't remember the name of it, but you'll know as a lover of books.

Sorry I can't be more helpful.

Right now, the most she reads are political books + articles.

Best wishes, Joan Baez, Sr.

Terry Gilliam

Director/Actor

Directorial film credits include *Time Bandits* and *Brazil*.
Starred in the *Monty Python* movies and television series.

Terry's Book List:

Brothers Karamazov
Catch 22
The Bible
Zen + The Art of Motorcycle Maintainance
Grimm's Fairytales
Philip K Dick's Androids Dream of Electric Sheep
Dante's Inferno
The Iliad
The Rebirth of Nature — Rupert Sheldrich   →

The latest collection of The Far Side
The Floating Opera — John Barth
The Third Policeman — O. Brian

The Art of Decorative Painting + Wallpaper

Hope your book goes well!

Best wishes,

Sharre Jacoby
(Terry's Assistant)

Hugh Downs

Broadcaster

Co-host of the *20/20* television program.

ABC News 20/20 157 Columbus Avenue New York NY 10023 (212) 580 6014

Hugh Downs

May 6, 1991

Dear Mr. Kelly:

Mr. Downs has asked me to reply to your recent letter and to send you a list of ten books he feels a well-educated person should read:

        Homer's "Iliad"
        The Bible
        Marcus Aurelius "Meditations"
        Cervantes "Don Quixote"
        Mark Twain's "Huckleberry Finn"
        Alexis de Toqueville's "Democracy in America"
        Shakespeare's works
        Fielding's "Tom Jones"
        Charles Darwin's "The Origin of the Species"
        U.S. Constitution

Also, regarding the greatest book he has ever read, Mr. Downs has elected "Northwest Passage" by Kenneth Roberts.

Thank you for your interest and please accept Mr. Downs' very best wishes.

Sincerely,

Jean Ferrari
Assistant to Mr. Downs

Barry Williams

Actor/Entertainer

Starred in the *Brady Bunch* television series.
Author of *Growing Up Brady: I Was A Teenage Greg.*

BARRY WILLIAMS
E N T E R P R I S E S

Monday, May 23, 1994

Dear Kevin:

Here's my pick list:

        10. A FAREWELL TO ARMS - Ernest Hemingway
         9. BRAVE NEW WORLD - Aldous Huxley
         8. CANDIDE - Voltaire
         7. MADAME BOVARY - G. Flaubert
         6. GREAT EXPECTATIONS - C. Dickens
         5. 1984 - G. Orwell
         4. MUSASHI - Eiji Yoshikawa
         3. SONS & LOVERS - D. H. Lawrence
         2. THE PROPHET - Kahil Gibran

and the most important book on any top 10 reading list in my opinion is .....

        #1. GROWING UP BRADY/I WAS A TEENAGE GREG

Good Luck!

Barry Williams

23679 Calabasas Road · Suite 124 · Calabasas · California · 91302

Clint Black

Musician/Entertainer

Album titles include *No Time To Kill*, *One Emotion*, and *Killin' Time*.

from the office of

CLINT BLACK

8489 WEST 3RD ST., 2ND FL. • LOS ANGELES, CALIFORNIA 90048
(213) 655-4423   FAX: (213) 655-2634

November 30, 1994

Dear Kevin:

In response to your request, the following are Clint Black's selections:

1. The Education of Little Tree
2. Silence of the Lambs
3. Forrest Gump
4. Fever Dream
5. The Bridges of Madison County
6. The Bible
7. Eat To Win
8. Kamakaze Cowboy
9. Where Is Joe Merchant?
10. Tales From Margaritaville

The greatest book he ever read? The Bible.

Best of luck with this project!

Sincerely,

Brenda Madison

BEM:rt

Edward Asner

Actor / Entertainer

Starred in the *The Mary Tyler Moore Show*, *Lou Grant*, and *Thunder Alley* television series.

Edward Asner

January 20, 1994

1. The Bible
2. The Prince/Machiavelli
3. Das Kapital
any book by the historians he read in college:
      4. Herodotus
      5. Thucydides
      6. Gibbon
7. Complete Works of William Shakespeare
8. The History of Western Civilization
9. The Economist
10. Theory of the Leisure Class
11. Candide
12. Babbitt
13. Brothers Karamazov

His Personal Favorite is:
      The Last of the Just by Andre Schwartz-Bart

Sincerely,

Paige Lipman
Assistant to Mr. Asner

encl: B/W pictures

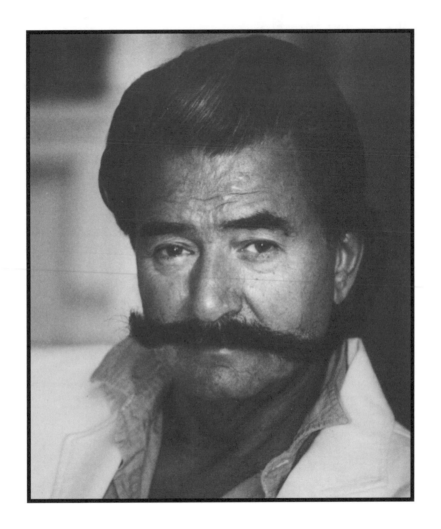

LeRoy Neiman

Artist

Impressionistic paintings of a wide variety of subjects.

LeROY NEIMAN   1 WEST 67TH ST.   NEW YORK, N.Y. 10023

I would like to suggest reading the writings of Mahatma Gandhi the preeminent leader of Indian Nationalism and the prophet of nonviolenence in the 20th Century. He wrote copiously the collected edition of his writing runs to more than 80 volumes.

Gandhi's autobiography -
The Story of My Experiences with Truth 1927-29

The Collected Works of Mahatma Gandhi 1958-84
includes all his writings, speeches and letters.

Gandhi's Seven Sins:

Wealth without Works
Pleasure without Conscience
Knowledge without Character
Commerce without Morality
Science without Humanity
Worship without Sacrifice
Politics without Principles

LeRoy Neiman 1/18/95

Garry Marshall

Director/Producer

Film credits include *Nothing in Common* and
The Flamingo Kid.

Garry K. Marshall
Henderson Prod. Co., Inc.

October 17, 1994

As requested, enclosed is Garry Marshall's signed "Permission to Publish and Reprint" and also the <u>REVISED</u> list of his ten favorite books, which are also listed below.   The photograph you requested is also enclosed.

1.   Mann's MAGIC MOUNTAIN
2.   Salinger's CATCHER IN THE RYE
3.   Hesse's SIDDHARTHA
4.   Flaubert's MADAME BOVARY
5.   Steinbeck's THE GRAPES OF WRATH
6.   Kafka's METAMORPHOSIS
7.   Shakespeare's HAMLET
8.   Nabokov's LOLITA
9.   Betty Friedan's FEMININE MYSTIQUE
10.   (a tie for 10th)   Moss Hart's ACT ONE
                         Ayn Rand's FOUNTAINHEAD

Thank you and good luck. I'm sending a copy of this letter to Kevin Kelly so he is aware of the revised list.

Sincerely,

Diane Frazen
Exec. Asst. to Garry Marshall

10067 RIVERSIDE DRIVE • TOLUCA LAKE, CA 91602

Peter Bogdanovich

Director

Film credits include *The Last Picture Show*, *Mask*, and *Paper Moon*.

PETER BOGDANOVICH

March 12, 1994

Dear Mr. Kelly:

Thank you for your letter to Mr. Bogdanovich concerning a list of his ten favorite books.

Mr. Bogdanovich wanted me to let you know that his favorite author is Mr. Robert Graves (who wrote over 150 books).

Again, thank you for your inquiry.

Sincerely,

September Bradford
Assistant to Mr. Bogdanovich

/sb

Don Ho

Musician

Best known for the song *Tiny Bubbles.*

HO ENTERPRISES LTD.

Dear Kevin,

This is a list of the greatest books I read that you requested.

1. Art Of War - Sun Tzu
2. In Search Of Excellence
3. Deming - Out Of The Crisis
4. Deming - Management Method
5. Rise And Fall Of Great Powers
6. Wealth Without Risk

Aloha,

Don Ho

2005 Kalia Road · Waikiki Beach, Hawaii 96815 · (808) 923-3981

Dear Mr. Kelly,

Thank you, belatedly, for your kind letter of January 24 to John Williams.

I spoke with Maestro Williams recently about your enormous questions regarding ten books that a well-read person should read. I'm afraid that his response came not in the form of titles but rather in the form of these categories: 20th Century French Literature, 19th Century English Literature, 19th and 20th Century American Literature, Greek plays, and Shakespeare, in addition to a large canon of religious and philosophical works.

As for the greatest book Maestro Williams had ever read, he had no answer. He is an extremely well-read person and it was impossible for him to pick a favorite or name one that had been the most influential on him.

Good luck with your book!

Very truly yours,

Diane M. Read
Assistant to the
Orchestra Manager

BOSTON SYMPHONY ORCHESTRA, INC.
SYMPHONY HALL, BOSTON, MASSACHUSETTS 02115
TELEPHONE: (617) 266-1492
FAX: (617) 266-9648

John Williams

Composer/Conductor

Scores include *E.T.*, the *Star Wars* series, and the *Indiana Jones* series. Head of the Boston Symphony Orchestra.

1. 100 Days of Sodom, Marquis De Sade
2. Pilgrim's Progress
3. Cat in the Hat
4. The Art of Dreaming (Castaneda)
5. Madame Bovary
6. Portnoy's Complaint
7. The Story of O
8. The Rise and Fall of the Third Reich
9. 1, Claudius
10. The Thorn Birds

Favorits : Lolita

I hope this is helpful

[signature]

Tony Bennett

Musician/Entertainer

Album titles include *Astoria, Best of Tony Bennett*, and
Tony Bennett-MTV Unplugged.

Heart & Souls
MCA/Universal Pictures

November 7, 1992

Dear Kevin:

I am sorry it has taken so long to respond to your simple request; however I am in pre-production and have been in the eye of a hurricane.

I would list the following books as significant to me:

> The Bible
> Moby Dick
> Gone With The Wind
> The History of Civilization
> Grapes of Wrath
> The Book of Tao
> The Old Man and the Sea
> Fahrenheit 451
> The Great Gatsby
> Hamlet

These are all books that have been important to me although I must admit that this list is quite arbitrary and my next month's list might be altogether different.

Hope this is some help to you on your project.

Best regards,

Ron Underwood

Ron Underwood

Director

Film credits include *City Slickers*, *Heart and Souls*, and *Tremors*.

Kevin, here's ten books that will give you a run for your money.

Cormac McCarthy: Blood Meridian
Dostoyevsky: Crime and Punishment
Henry Miller: Black Spring
Louis F. Celine: Journey to the End of the Night
Miyamoto Mushashi: A Book of Five Rings
Hubert Selby: The Room
Nelson Algren: Somebody in Boots
Albert Camus: The Plague
Yukio Mishima: Confessions of a Mask
Knut Hamsun: Mysteries

Greatest book I ever read. Nietzsche: Thus Spoke Zarathustra

OK, there you go.

H. Rollins

Henry Rollins

Musician/Writer

Former leadsinger of Black Flag and currently the frontman
for the Henry Rollins Band. Author of *Get in the Van*.

10-6-1991

DEAR KEVIN,

I AM SORRY TO INFORM YOU THAT I HAVE NOT EVEN READ MORE THAN TEN BOOKS. UNLESS YOU COUNT COMIC BOOKS.

ANYWAY I DO RECALL BEING INFLUENCED BY THE FOLLOWING BOOKS:

BEING THERE BY JERZY KOSINSKI

ART OF THE DEAL BY DONALD TRUMP

VARIOUS BOOKS BY ANDY WARHOL.

BELIEVE IT OR NOT, I HAVE AUTHORED MORE BOOKS THAN I HAVE READ AND I AM CURRENTLY BEING VERY INFLUENCED BY MY LATEST BOOK KOSTABI: THE EARLY YEARS PLEASE SEND ME A CHECK FOR $225. AND I'LL SEND YOU A SIGNED COPY.

THANK YOU — MARK KOSTABI

544 WEST 38TH STREET NEW YORK NY 10018 (212) 268 0616 FAX 268-7119

Mark Kostabi

Artist/Entrepreneur

Professional Artist and head of Kostabi World.

TONIGHT

TONIGHT SHOW
3000 West Alameda Avenue • Burbank, CA 91523 • (818) 840-3691

ED McMAHON

May 21, 1991

Dear Kevin:

Thanks for your letter and for including me in your project. The greatest book I have ever read is **THE PROPHET** *by Kahlil Gibran. Others in my top ten would include* **THE BOURNE IDENTITY** *or anything by Robert Ludlum,* **THE HUNT FOR RED OCTOBER,** *and I would have to include the classic* **TREASURE ISLAND.** *I hope this helps and good luck with your book!*

All good wishes.

Cordially,

ED McMAHON

Ed McMahon

Host/Entertainer

Host of television's *Star Search* and former co-host of *The Tonight Show.*

March 21, 1991

Dear Kevin:

Following is a list of the ten books that have had the
greatest impact on me (though if you asked me on another day
the list would probably be very different):

> Joseph Heller's "Catch-22"
> Voltaire's "Candide"
> Terry Sothern, "The Magic Christian"
> Albert Camus' "The Stranger"
> Franz Kafka's "The Castle"
> James Joyce's "The Dubliners"
>   (for pure prose beauty)
> William Sergeant's "The Battle for the Mind"
> Ralph Ellison's "The Invisible Man"
> Freud's "Civilization and Its Discontents"
> Cervantes' "Don Quixote"

I would have to say that the greatest book I have ever read
is "Candide."

Best of luck with your book; it's certainly an interesting
idea.

Regards,

Wes Craven

Wes Craven

Director

Film credits include the *A Nightmare on Elm Street* series,
The Hills Have Eyes, and *Deadly Friend*.

Hi Kevin

DA

1) Crisis of the Negro
   Intellectual – Harold Cruise

2) They Came Before
   Columbus –
        Ivan Van Sertima

(3 Autobiography of
    Malcolm X

4) The Prophet – Khalil
            Gibran

5.) Cultural Literacy
      E. D. Hirsch

6.) Invisible Man
     Ralph Ellison

7.) Essays James Baldwin

DA

8.) Iliad + the
    Odyssey by
    Homer

9.) Aristotle's Poetics

10.) MacBeth –
     Shakespeare

     Good Luck

     Debbie
     Allen

Debbie Allen

Choreographer / Entertainer

Choreographed countless award shows, music videos, and musicals. Starred in the *Fame* movie and television series. Currently stars in the *In the House* television series.

Bill Conti

Composer/Conductor

Composer and Conductor for the Academy Awards.
First person to respond to my letter.

BILL CONTI
c/o Freedman, Kinzelberg & Broder
2121 Avenue of the Stars, Suite 900
Los Angeles, Calif. 90067

January 31, 1991

Dear Kevin:

Your book sounds very interesting. In response to your request for
my favorite books, I can tell you that I prefer books of philosophy.
I read a lot of Mortimer Adler, including How to Think About God,
Reforming Education, and Aristotle for Everybody. Joseph Campbell
is another author I greatly admire, especially his books Myths to
Live By and The Hero with a Thousand Faces.

Other books that I recommend include Unlimited Power by Anthony
Robbins; The Trial of Socrates by I. F. Stone; In Patagonia by
Bruce Chatwin; and my personal greatest book, Levels of Knowing and
Existence by Harry Weinberg.

Hope that helps.

Yours truly,

Bill Conti

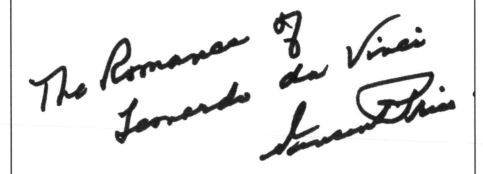

Vincent Price

Actor /Entertainer/Director

Film credits include *The House of Wax*, *Edward Scissorhands*, and *The Abominable Doctor Phibes*.

1. Zen + the Art of Motorcycle Maint —
2. Iron John
3. The Bible
4. Siddartha
5. Richard II
6. Tale of Two Citys
7. Golf in the Kingdom
8. Lord of the Rings
9. Scarlet letter —
10. Dr. Jekyl + Mr Hyde

Craig T. Nelson

Actor / Entertainer

Stars in the *Coach* television series. Film credits include the *Poltergeist* series.

Rememberance of Things Past

Zen and the Art of Archery

War and Peace

Secret Garden

Anything by Edith Warton

History of the English Speaking People by Winston C.

favorite book

War + Peace

Good luck!

Joan Rivers

Comedian/Entertainer/Author

Hosted the *Joan Rivers Show*. Author of *Enter Talking, Still Talking*, and *The Life and Hard Times of Heidi Abromowitz*.

I'm not sure I could properly identify the "greatest" book I've ever read as you requested. I can only tell you that the "Autobiography of Malcolm X" is the book that had the greatest impact on my life. To a young black man growing up on Chicago's South Side, the book was a revelation, prompting me to look at myself and my world as I'd never done before.

Bryant C. Gumbel
Host
NBC's Today Show

Bryant C. Gumbel

Host

Host of NBC's *Today Show*.

"All good books are alike in that they are truer than if they really happen and after you finished reading one you will feel that it all happened to you, and afterwards it all belongs to you."

Ernest Hemingway,
An Old Newsman Writes

EXECUTIVES
AND
NOTABLES

Helen Gurley Brown

Editor

Editor-In-Chief of *Cosmopolitan* magazine.

COSMOPOLITAN

Helen Gurley Brown, Editor · 224 West 57th Street, New York, New York, 10019, (212) 649-3555

February 27, 1991

Dear Mr. Kelly,

What a super project. I wish I could be more
helpful but I'm not desperately "literary" and it
would take me two or three days to come up with a
list of books I think a well read person should
read!!! I don't know the greatest book I ever read.
My favorite book was Gone With The Wind which shows
you the shape we are in terms of being helpful. My
second favorite book was The Godfather. I don't
think I read anything that helped in my career
though other people certainly have. Thanks for
thinking of me -- sorry I can't be more helpful.

All my best wishes,

Helen B.

HGB/rc

P.S. My letter sounds really flip! Don't mean it
to. If I had read a bit more, I might have started
my life work as an editor before age 43!

Peter Bahouth

Environmentalist

Former head of *Greenpeace USA*.

ADELAIDE • AMSTERDAM • ANCHORAGE • AUCKLAND • BOSTON • BRUSSELS • BUENOS AIRES • CHICAGO • COPENHAGEN • DUBLIN
FORT LAUDERDALE • GOTHENBERG • HAMBURG • LEWES — U.K. • LONDON • LUXEMBOURG • MADRID • MONTREAL • OSLO • PALMA DE MALLORCA
PARIS • ROME • SAN FRANCISCO • SAN JOSE — COSTA RICA • SEATTLE • STOCKHOLM • SYDNEY • TORONTO • VANCOUVER • VIENNA
WASHINGTON • WORLD PARK BASE — ANTARCTICA • ZURICH

GREENPEACE

Greenpeace USA • 1436 U Street NW • Washington DC 20009 • Tel (202) 462-1177
Tlx 89-2359 • Fax (202) 462-4507

April 25, 1991

Dear Mr. Kelly:

Thank you for your recent letter. I apologize for the delay in responding, but I have been travelling for the past several weeks.

I appreciate your asking for my opinion, but it would be difficult for me to say what a well-read and well-educated person should read. I can, however, give you a very brief list of some of my favorites:

* Making Peace with the Planet
* Population Explosion
* State of the World (put out by the World Watch Institute)
* Hazardous Waste in America (by Ralph Nader)
* Silent Spring (by Rachel Carson)

I hope that these choices will help you in your work. Good luck and I wish you much success with your book.

Sincerely,

Peter Bahouth
Executive Director

RECYCLED PAPER

J. Warren Cassidy

Director

Former Director of the National Rifle Association of America.

NATIONAL RIFLE ASSOCIATION OF AMERICA
INCORPORATED 1871
1600 RHODE ISLAND AVENUE, N.W.
WASHINGTON, D.C. 20036

J. WARREN CASSIDY

30 July, '91

Dear Kevin,

Please forgive the overly long dealy in my response to your
request of 29 May '91. I resigned from NRA at the end of
February, moved to New Hampshire in June (after selling our
Virginia home in May) and have been busy ever since in preparing
our former vacation home for year 'round use.

In the event you are still interested, I submit the following
list in no particular order;

Conquests by Man -Paul Herrman (probably mispelled)
the Patriot Lad series (author forgotten)
Boy Scout Handbook
One Hundred One Famous Poems - anthology, Roy Jay Cook, 1929
A Stillness at Appomattox - Bruce Catton
Hamlet
Guadalcanal Diary - Richard Tregaskis
Grapes of Wrath - Steinbeck
Tobacco Road - Erskine Caldwell
The Declaration of Independence & The Constitution of the U.S.

These may not fit your requirement of "books" but they are the
works to which I've most referred and that most influenced me.

Good luck on your book.

Sincerely,

Pat Robertson

Evangelist

Chairman of the Board of the Christian Broadcasting Network.

BOOKS THAT SHAPED SUCCESSFUL PEOPLE

CBN CENTER VIRGINIA BEACH, VIRGINIA 23463 (804) 424-7777

The Christian Broadcasting Network Inc.

Pat Robertson
CHAIRMAN OF THE BOARD
CHIEF EXECUTIVE OFFICER

July 22, 1991

Dear Kevin:

Thank you for your letter and your interest in reading books that knowledgeable people read.

I will give you a couple of books which I consider among the most important books I have ever read. Time does not permit me to give you 10 as you requested.

The one, outside of the Bible, that has most influenced my life is:
<u>With Christ in the School of Prayer</u>, by Andrew Murray.

Others are: <u>The Practice of the Presence of God</u>, by Brother Lawrence.

<u>Revivals of Religion</u>, by Charles G. Finney.

The book that I consider the best I have personally authored is <u>The Secret Kingdom</u>, published by Thomas Nelson Publishers.

I hope this is helpful. May God bless you. I am

Sincerely,

Pat Robertson
Chairman of the Board
Chief Executive Officer

PR:bj

Henry Bloch

CEO

Chairman and Chief Executive Officer of H&R Block.

H&R Block, Inc.
Corporate Headquarters
4410 Main Street
Kansas City, Missouri 64111

(816) 932-8413

Henry W. Bloch
Chairman and
Chief Executive Officer

March 21, 1991

Dear Mr. Kelly:

I received your interesting inquiry about my reading habits. My time is quite limited and I find what time is available for reading gets devoted solely to current periodicals. My leisure time centers around my wife, my family, my community and a little bit of tennis. Occasionally, I will scan a book on a casual basis, but I have very little time to sit down and enjoy a good "read."

I know of no book that has had a greater influence on the people whom I know other than the primary religious texts, such as the Bible and the Torah. The concepts of values and ethics embodied there are the ones I feel most strongly permeate daily business activities and most significantly influence the conduct of business.

I wish you well with your project and hope you will be successful in your endeavors.

Very truly yours,

Henry W. Bloch

HWB:TJ

Harold A. Poling

CEO

Chairman of the Board and Chief Executive
Officer (Retired) of Ford Motor Company.

Harold A. Poling
Chairman of the Board
and Chief Executive Officer
(Retired)

Regent Court Building
Suite 1080
16800 Executive Plaza Drive
Dearborn, Michigan 48126

March 2, 1994

Dear Mr. Kelly:

I am pleased to help you with your book by providing you with a
list of suggested reading.

The "greatest" book I read and one of my favorite was "Advise
and Consent by Allen Drury, and the list continues with "At
Dawn We Slept" by Gordon Prange, "Head to Head" by Lester
Thurow, "Truman" by David McCullough, "American Caesar" by
William Manchester, "The Power Game" by Hedrick Smith,
"Speaking My Mind" by Ronald Reagan, "Special Envoy" by W.
Averell Harriman and Elie Abel, "The Triumph of Politics" by
Daniel Stockman, "The Downing Street Years" by Margaret
Thatcher, "President Kennedy" by Richard Reeves and "Jimmy
Carter-The Man & The Myth" by Victor Lasky.

For relaxation, I enjoy books written by authors Tom Clancy,
Allen Drury, and Robert Ludlum.

I wish you success with the publication of your book.

Sincerely,

H. A. Poling

Sri Easwaran

Spiritual Leader

Head of the Blue Mountain Center of Meditation.
Author of countless books and spiritual translations.

Blue Mountain Center of Meditation / Nilgiri Press

P.O. Box 256, Tomales, California 94971 / Telephone: 707 878–2369

February 8, 1994

Dear Kevin Kelly,

Thank you for your recent letter regarding the research you are doing. Sri Easwaran was an English Professor in India before he took to the spiritual life and can appreciate your work on the book in question. Here are the titles of the ten books Sri Easwaran listed:

The Bhagavad Gita
The Upanishads
THE IMITATION OF CHRIST by Thomas a Kempis
PARADISE LOST by John Milton
AN AUTOBIOGRAPHY by M.K. Gandhi
ANNA KARENINA by Leo Tolstoy
MAN AND SUPERMAN by George Bernard Shaw
SHAKUNTALA by Kalidasa (translated by Binyon)
TOWARD FREEDOM by Jawaharlal Nehru (his autobiography)
The Essays of Ralph Waldo Emerson

The book he would place above all is the Bhagavad Gita. He has published his own translation, as well as a three-volume commentary, on this scripture.

With all good wishes for the success of your work,

Sincerely,

Melissa Larson

Melissa Larson

Joan Embery

Goodwill Ambassador/Author

Serves as Goodwill Ambassador for the Zoological Society of San Diego, Author of four books including *My Wild World* and *Amazing Animal Facts*.

The Zoological Society of San Diego

April 8, 1991

Dear Mr. Kelly,

In response to your recent letter, due to Joan's hectic schedule she does not have time to read many books but Joan has read many periodicals and newspaper articles in order to keep informed and current on topics related to her field of animals and the environment.

The following list is of the periodicals Joan reads on a regular basis:

USA Today
Zoo Life
Christian Science Monitor
National Wildlife
International Wildlife
AAZPA Comminque

One of the main sources in book form Joan uses for her animal information is:

Grzimek's Animal Life Encyclopedia
Grzimek's Encyclopedia of Ecology

Sincerely,

Janet Tuttle

Janet Tuttle
Assistant to the Goodwill Ambassador

Post Office Box 551, San Diego, California 92112-0551 USA Telephone (619) 231-1515 FAX (619) 231-0249

Richard M. Rosenberg

CEO

Chairman and Chief Executive Officer of Bank of America.

Bank of America

Richard M. Rosenberg
Chairman and
Chief Executive Officer

March 21, 1991

Dear Kevin:

Thank you for your letter regarding what a well-read and well-educated person should read.

My favorite book is <u>Hunt for Red October</u>, and following is a list of books that I feel everyone should read:

> Iliad
> Odyssey
> Images of the Cave by Plato
> Poetics by Aristotle
> The Prophet by Gibran
> On Liberty by John Stuart Mill
> Freedom at Midnight
> Alexis deTocqueville, essays and observations on visits to the
>   United States
> Life of Churchill
> Night by Elie Weisel
> Gone with the Wind

Sincerely,

RMR:pl

Bank of America National Trust and Savings Association Box 37000 San Francisco, California 94137

Henry Luce III

Executive

Former Director of Time Warner, Inc.

from the desk of   HENRY LUCE III

Greatest Book: The Bible

Books of greatest influence:
The Bible
Shakespearean Tragedies
Witness, by Whitaker Chambers
Huckleberry Finn, by
Mark Twain

The Statesman
The Prince, by Machiavelli
Arrowsmith, by Sinclair Lewis
The Federalist, by John Adams,
John Jay, + James Madison

THE HENRY LUCE FOUNDATION, INC.

Sincerely yours, Henry Luce III

Jason McManus

Executive

Former Director of Time Warner, Inc.

TO: Kevin Kelly

FROM: Jason McManus

DATE: November 28, 1994

1.   The Bible

2.   Homer's The Iliad

3.   Plato's Republic

4.   Aristotle's Ethics

5.   Locke's Essay Concerning Human Understanding

6.   Shakespeare's history plays

7.   Tolstoy's War and Peace

8.   Alexis de Tocqueville's Democracy in America

9.   Oscar Wilde's The Importance of Being Earnest

10. F. Scott Fitzgerald's The Great Gatsby

     The greatest: War and Peace

Gloria Steinem

Feminist/Author

Author of *Moving Beyond Words* and *Revolution from Within*.
Co-founded *Ms*. magazine.

Gloria Steinem

17 November 1994

Thank you for your letter to Gloria and for including her in your project. She is busy keeping up with her various commitments, but asked me to respond for her.

Following are ten books that have affected Gloria's life and ones that should be shared with other people:

<u>Little Women</u> - by Louisa May Alcott

<u>Backlash</u> - by Susan Faludi

<u>This Bridge Called My Back: Writings by Radical Women of Color</u> - by Cherrie Moraga and Gloria Anzaldua.

<u>Refusing to Be a Man</u> - by John Stoltenberg

<u>If Women Counted</u> - by Marilyn Waring

<u>The Color Purple</u> - by Alice Walker

<u>The Creation of Patriarchy</u> - by Gerda Lerner

<u>The Chalice and The Blade</u> - by Riane Eisler

<u>Invented Lives: Narratives of Black Women 1860-1960</u> - by Mary Helen Washington

<u>Sisterhood is Global</u> - by Robin Morgan

This list is by no means extensive. Gloria has read many great books, but for the purpose of your book, let's say that <u>Little Women</u> is the greatest book she has ever read.

Good luck with your project and thank you again for thinking of Gloria.

Sincerely,

Amy Richards

25 March, 1995

Dear Kevin Kelly,

Here is a response to your letter about books. Since I scribbled my first reply, I have spent some time thinking about books. And I find it impossible to chose just ten books! Because there are so MANY books that would be left out that, if a person had not read them, we would NOT think he was properly educated. So I have rewritten my response, and organized my list into ten *categories* of books!

1. Religion and philosophy. The well educated Christian, Jew, Muslim, Budhist, etc obviously needs to read the religious writings of his or her particular faith. THE *BIBLE* is on my list not only for this reason, but because it is full of stories, full of history - it is good entertainment value, in addition to everything else. The well educated person needs to know *something* about the other major religions.

2. SHAKESPEARE. *The Works of William Shakespeare* (whoever wrote them!) No English speaking person could be considered well educated if he or she has not read Hamlet, Macbeth, the Merchant of Venice, Julius Caesar, and so on. I think Goethe probably ranks along with Shakespear.

3. Historical/ social issues novels. One of Charles Dickens, perhaps *DAVID COPPERFIELD* or *Oliver Twist*. *Uncle Tom's Cabin*. *Cry the Beloved Country*. *The Tree that Grew in Brooklyn* (I'm not sure if that is the correct title?). One of Alexander Solzhenitsyn's powerful novels, perhaps *THE FIRST CIRCLE*.

4. Historical, Non-fiction. Winston Churchill's *THE SECOND WORLD WAR - VOL 1. THE GATHERING STORM*. (If one is English). Or perhaps his *History of the English Speaking People*. One should at least know something about Gibbons *Decline and Fall of the Roman Empire*.

5. True Science/Adventure Rachel Carson's *SILENT SPRING*. And one should know about Charles Darwin's *The Voyage of the Beagle* or *The Descent of Man*. *The Kon Tiki Expedition* by Thor Heyadahl.

6. The Classics. One must read at least one of Jane Austin's novels - *Pride and Predjudice*, for example. And an educated English person MUST have read Charlotte Bronte's *JANE EYRE* and her sister's *WUTHERING HEIGHTS*. Thomas Hardy - perhaps *Far from the Madding Crowd*. Robert Louis Stevenson: *Treasure Island*. And an American must be familiar with Faulkner.

Jane Goodall

Chimpanzee expert

Author of *In the Shadow of Man* and *My Life with the Chimpanzees*. Head of Gombe Wildlife Research Institute.

7. Children's classics - the books you read or have read to you as a child and enjoy (usually in different way) as an adult. Lewis Carrol's *ALICE IN WONDERLAND;* James Barrie's *PETER PAN;* A. A. Milne's *WINNIE THE POOH;* Rudyard Kipling's *JUST SO STORIES;* Kenneth Graham's *WIND IN THE WILLOWS.* And *The Water Babies* (only I don't remember the author). *Black Beauty.* (author?) And next, those children's books that are more or less confined to childhood, yet so often referred to in adult life. Such as *ANDERSON AND GRIMM'S FAIRY TALES.* I mean, you have to know about *Jack and the Beanstalk* and *the Snow Queen* and *Rumplestiltskin,* don't you? And Beatrix Potter - *THE TALE OF PETER RABBIT* for example.

8. Poetry. Because, to be well educated you need to have read something of many different poets, and because it is not possible to chose one over another except as a personal preference (nothing to do with being well-educaated!) I have to suggest, horror of horrors! - an anthology. But a really good, long, ANTHOLOGY - of poetry down the ages.

9. Miscellaneous. There are certain authors that a well educated person needs to have heard of, needs a nodding acquaintance with. I would include George Bernard Shaw, Paul Satre, Camus, Somerset Maugham, Saki, etc. And surely one needs to know who Hercule Poirot is, or Sherlock Holmes - or even Perry Mason!

10. Books that just happened to be special for me (just to make the ten categories!) Two books - series of books actually - that profoundly affected my own life - sent me to Africa. The *Doctor Doolittle* books, good old Hugh Lofting. And, of course, Edgar Rice Burroughs *TARZAN!* And I adore *The Lord of the Rings.* And two novels, a story in two parts, by Laurens vander Post, *A Story Like the Wind* and *A Far-Off Place.*

The above list is terribly inadequate. I decided to leave it there, because otherwise it would get very long, and each time I look it through I get sense of outrage - how could I have ommitted THAT book, or THIS book! And so the list would become absurd! Even with the above list, I am far from answering your question!

Jane Goodall.

GENTLEMEN'S QUARTERLY

Arthur Cooper, Editor-in-Chief (212) 880-7915

December 9, 1994

Dear Kevin,

Here, in no particular order, is my top ten list:

The Great Gatsby by F. Scott Fitzgerald
The Sun Also Rises by Ernest Hemingway
Catch-22 by Joseph Heller — *my favorite book*
David Copperfield by Charles Dickens
Truman by David McCullough
African Genesis by Robert Ardrey
The Rise and Fall of the Third Reich by William Shirer
Case Closed by Gerald Posner
Battle Cry of Freedom by James M. McPherson
Lincoln by Gore Vidal

I wish you the best of luck with your book.

Art Cooper

Arthur Cooper

Editor

Editor-in-Chief of *Gentlemen's Quarterly* magazine.

A Dance to the Music of Time
Anthony Powell

Flashman and The Pirates
George MacDonald Fraser

A Child of the Century
Ben Hecht

Act One
Moss Hart.

This is New York
E. B. White

Lucky Jim
Kingsley Amis

Huckleberry Finn
Mark Twain

Right Ho, Jeeves'
P. G. Wodehouse

A Catcher in The Rye
J. D. Salinger

The Glory & the Dream
William Manchester.

E. Graydon Carter

Editor

Editor-in-Chief of *Vanity Fair* magazine.

"Reading is to the mind what exercise

is to the body."

Richard Steele, *The Tatler*

SPORTS

Bob Costas

Sportscaster/Entertainer

Hosted *Later with Bob Costas*. Currently broadcasts sports for the National Broadcasting Company.

Kevin - You realize this is impossible! Good Luck! (*signed*) Bob Costas

The Bible (or the Baseball Encyclopedia)
The Odyssey - Homer
Huckleberry Finn - Twain
King Lear, Hamlet, or Macbeth - Willie S.
Invisible Man - Ralph Ellison
Catcher in the Rye - J. D. Salinger
The Sound and the Fury - Wm. Faulkner
Grapes of Wrath - John Steinbeck
A Good Anthology of English Language Poetry
The Naked & The Dead - Norman Mailer
Feminine Mystique - Betty Friedan

Personal: "Mickey Mantle: Mr. Yankee" - Gene Schoor
(*Read at age 8. Still a classic to this day.*)

Hey Kevin - probably some Sartre & Camus plus some Freud & Jung wouldn't hurt...but who do I look like...Alistair Cooke?

11/8/94

In glancing at my list I noticed that Aristotle, Plato, Tolstoy, Hemingway, Fitzgerald, Proust, Whitman, Joyce, Cervantes & Jane Austen are among the missing - I must have been in a hurry that day - or perhaps it was before I finished my Hooked on Phonics course.

BC

Lou Holtz

Coach

Head Coach of the Notre Dame football team.

University of Notre Dame

Football Office

Lou Holtz
Head Football Coach

April 3, 1991

Dear Kevin:

Thank you for your letter inquiring about the books I feel are
very special and should be read. Following are my selections:

1. The Bible (greatest book)

2. Magic of Thinking Big by David Schwartz

3. See You At The Top by Zig Ziglar

4. The Be Happy Attitudes by Dr. Robert Schuller

5. Tough Times Don't Last, Tough People Do
   by Dr. Robert Schuller

Best wishes in your endeavors.

Sincerely,

LOU HOLTZ

ks

Joyce Athletic and Convocation Center • Post Office Box 518, Notre Dame, Indiana 46556

Chris Evert

Tennis Champion

Winner of six U.S. Open tennis single titles and a four time
Wimbledon singles champion.

EVERT ENTERPRISES/IMG

10 April 1991

Dear Kevin,

There are three books that stand out as ones I think a well read person should read, and they are: <u>The Fountainhead</u>; <u>Prince of Tides</u> and <u>Lie Down with the Lions.</u>

Thank you for your letter, and best of luck with your book.

Sincerely,

Chris Evert

Chris Evert

CE:mlh
cc:J. Evert
   B. Kain

7100 West Camino Real, Suite 203, Boca Raton, Florida 33433 USA
Telephone: (407) 394-2400   Fax (407) 394-2479

Arnold Palmer

Professional Golfer

Four time winner of the Masters Golf Tournament as well as numerous other golf titles.

7/10/91

Dear Kevin: Mr. Palmer is out of the country for the next two weeks. I am responding to your request on his behalf.

Listed below are a few of Mr. Palmer's favorite books:

THE POWER OF POSITIVE THINKING
A TIME FOR ACTION

Hope this will help you out on your book you are doing.

Thanks for writing.

Debbie Rusnock
ARNOLD PALMER ENTERPRISES

Dave Anderson

Sports Journalist/Author

Sportswriter for *The New York Times*. Author of *The Sport of Basketball* and *In the Corner:Great Boxing Trainers Talk*.

Dear Kevin:

My top ten --   Shakespeare's plays
                The Bible
                Hemingway's Old Man and the Sea
                Dickens' Oliver Twist
                any Red Smith collection
                Mark Twain's Tom Sawyer/Huckleberry Finn
                Dan Jenkins' Semi-Tough
                William L. Shirer's Berlin Diary
                whatever James Michener book appeals to you
                Baseball Encyclopedia

Greatest book -- too many to mention one, but if you
                 insist "Old Man and the Sea"

                      Best,

                      Dave Anderson

Kevin Kelly –
Timberline by Gene Fowler
War and Peace – Tolstoi
Anthony Adverse – Hervey Allen?
Billy the Kid – Walter Noble Burns
Buddenbrooks – Thomas Mann
Such Interesting People – Bob Casey
Any Hemingway – No Faulkner
Joseph Attababla Series on Civil War

Jim Murray

Sports Journalist/Author

Sportswriter for *The Los Angeles Times*. Author of the
Jim Murray Collection.

Ray C. Leonard
T/A Sugar Ray Leonard

Personal Secretary
Caren L. Kinder

July 18, 1991

Dear Mr. Kelly:

Ray Leonard has had an opportunity to review your letter
requesting a list of his ten most influential books.
He asked me to relay this list to you as follows:

1. Kaffir Boy in America
2. Ray Charles
3. Mickey Rooney
4. There Are No Children Here
5. The Little Prince
6. Unlimited Powers
7. Josephine Baker (Bio)
8. Gordon Parks (Bio)
9. Voices of Freedom
10. The Prophet

The first one listed is his favorite. Mr. Leonard
appreciates your thinking of him and wishes you happy
reading!

Very truly yours,

Caren L. Kinder

CLK:jh
7003

Ray C. Leonard

Boxing Champion

Former Welterwieght Champion of the world.

"Literature… becomes the living

memory of a nation."

**Aleksandr Solzhenitsyn, from his
Nobel Prize acceptance speech, 1972**

WRITERS

Allen Ginsberg

Poet/Author

Author of *Howl, and Other Poems, Cosmopolitan Greetings,* and *Kaddish, and Other Poems.*

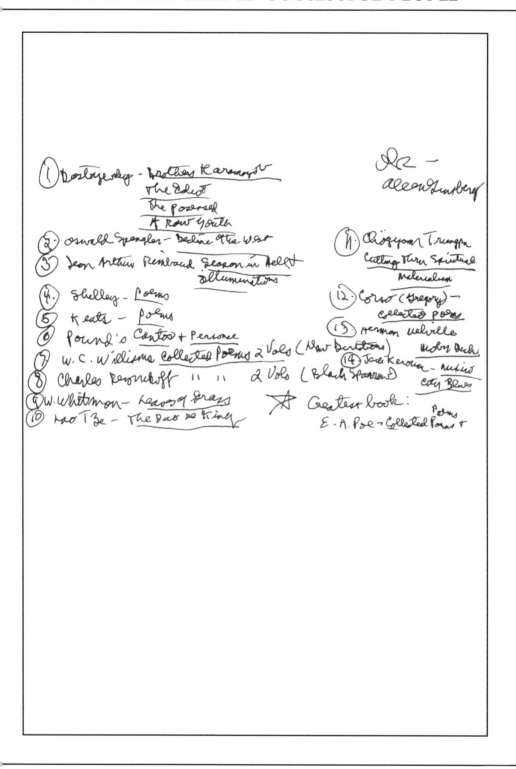

AG —
Allen Ginsberg

1. Dostoyevsky — Brothers Karamazov
   The Idiot
   The Possessed
   A Raw Youth
2. Oswald Spengler — Decline of the West
3. Jean Arthur Rimbaud Season in Hell
   Illuminations
4. Shelley — Poems
5. Keats — Poems
6. Pound's Cantos + Personae
7. W. C. Williams Collected Poems 2 Vols (New Directions)
8. Charles Reznikoff " " 2 Vols (Black Sparrow)
9. W. Whitman — Leaves of Grass
10. Mao Tze — The Dao De King

11. Chögyam Trungpa
    Cutting Thru Spiritual
    Materialism
12. Corso (Gregory) —
    Collected Poems
13. Herman Melville
    Moby Dick
14. Jack Kerouac — Mexico
    City Blues

☆ Greatest book:
   E. A. Poe — Collected Poems +

Dean Koontz

Writer

Author of *Watchers, Lightning,* and *Dark Rivers of the Heart.*

DEAN KOONTZ

16 October 1994

VIA FAX -- THIS PAGE ONLY

Thank you for your letter of 11 October, regarding <u>What successful People Read</u> by Kevin Kelly.

I'd like to amend the handwritten note I sent him, and I hereby give you permission to print the following:

> I can't list just ten books that a well-educated person should have read, for there are hundreds. Likewise, I can't identify a "best" book, because each book is different and can't be compared to others. In my estimation, however, <u>A Tale of Two Cities</u> should be on everyone's list because of what it has to say about the evil of large political movements and the triumph of the individual spirit over the tyranny of the mob--which is particularly pertinent in this age of political correctness. And I'd include <u>Huckleberry Finn</u> for its acerbic wit and <u>To Kill a Mockingbird</u> for its gentle wit--and both books for their powerful indictment of bigotry and for the great faith that they place in the effectiveness of individual conscience.

I hope this longer version--and the addition of one title--gives you no problem. The original response was off-the-cuff but still pretty close to what I'd say with more consideration.

Sincerely,

Dean Koontz

Post Office Box 9529, Newport Beach, California 92658-9529
Telephone 714 644-0943 Fax 714 644-4766

Anna Quindlen

Columnist/Author

Former New York Times syndicated columnist. Author of *Living Out Loud*, *Object Lessons*, and *One True Thing*.

The New York Times
229 WEST 43 STREET
NEW YORK, N.Y. 10036

ANNA QUINDLEN
Columnist

1. Bleak House
2. Pride and Prejudice
3. War and Peace
4. Complete Works of William Shakespeare
5. Collected Works of Yeats
6. The Sound and the Fury
7. To Kill a Mockingbird
8. Little Women
9. The Lion, The Witch and The Wardrobe
10. Middlemarch

Greatest? Tie: 1 and 10.

Day of The Jackal

— Forsyth

Tom Clancy

Writer

Author of *Red Storm Rising*, *The Hunt For Red October*,
and *Patriot Games*.

I don't go along with the idea that books shape successful people in any dominant way. The books which shaped me the most were the volumes of Compton's Pictured Encyclopedia which I got for my birthday at age 11 and read through from Aardvark to Zygote.

Robert Pirsig

Writer

Author of *Zen and the Art of Motorcycle Maintenance*, and *Lila: An Inquiry into Morals*.

Sidney Sheldon

Writer

Author of *Bloodline*, *The Doomsday Conspiracy*, and *Rage of Angels*.

Sidney Sheldon

October 23, 1991

Dear Mr. Kelly:

Your letter has been forwarded to me by my publisher, William Morrow & Company.

In answer to your inquiry:

The works of James Thurber
The works of Robert Benchley
Life With Father by Clarence Day
Rebecca by Daphne du Maurier
Gone With The Wind by Margaret Mitchell
Of Human Bondage by W. Somerset Maugham
The Web and The Rock of Time and The River by Thomas Wolfe
A Connecticut Yankee by Mark Twain
Perhaps I'll Dream of Darkness by Mary Sheldon (a personal favorite of mine)

Happy reading!

Sincerely,

ss/b

Jackie Collins

Writer

Author of *Hollywood Wives*, *Chances*, and *Rock Star*.

JACKIE COLLINS

Dear Kevin,

Thank you so much for your nice letter. I really appreciate hearing from readers who enjoy my books. I have fun writing them, and I am pleased to hear that you have fun reading them.

My new book, LADY BOSS, is in the stores now, it is a sequel to CHANCES and LUCKY, the continuing adventures of Lucky and Gino Santangelo.

Keep on reading!

Best wishes,

Jackie Collins

The greatest book I've ever read and everyone should read is THE GREAT GATSBY by F. Scott Fitzgerald!!

Mortimer Adler

Writer/Philosopher

Author of *The American Testament*, *Aristotle for Everybody*,
and *How to Speak, How to Listen*.

LIST OF RECOMMENDED WORKS BY MORTIMER ADLER

Thucydides: <u>The History of the Peloponnesian War</u>

Plato: <u>The Republic</u>

Aristotle: <u>Nicomachean Ethics</u> *and* <u>Politics</u>

St. Augustine: <u>The Confessions</u>

Plutarch: <u>The Lives of the Noble Grecians and Romans</u>

Saint Thomas Aquinas: "Treatise on God" (<u>Summa Theologica</u>)

Marcus Aurelius: <u>The Meditations</u>

Montaigne: <u>The Essays</u>

Pascal: <u>Pensees</u>

Shakespeare: The Tragedies

John Locke: <u>Concerning Civil Government, Second Essay</u>

J. S. Mill: <u>Representative Government</u>

William James: <u>The Principles of Psychology</u>

Jonathan Swift: <u>Gulliver's Travels</u>

Sigmund Freud

Mary Higgins Clark

Writer

Author of *The Anastasia Syndrome*, *All Around the Town*, and *The Lottery Winner*.

Dear Kevin —

There simply aren't any <u>ten</u>.

Off the top of my head, start with Shakespeare, (I know we're talking plays but more than that we're talking <u>reading</u>.)

<u>The Good Earth</u> / Isaac B Singer (just about anything) Joyce, (anything) The Republic, Les Miserables—

on and on we go — The point is one keeps on reading, then rereads the classics —

And don't forget <u>Gone With the Wind</u> —

I don't know if that's much help but it's like asking the mother of many to name her favorite kids.

Best,

Mary Higgins Clark

M. Scott Peck

Writer

Author of *The Road Less Traveled* and *Further Along
the Road Less Traveled.*

M. Scott Peck

July 26, 1991

Dear Kevin:

Dr. Peck thanks you for your recent request. Because of the enormous volume of requests coming his way, he cannot take the time to list books for you but will let you know that his very favorite book of all time is C.S. Lewis' book <u>Till We Have Faces</u>.

Most sincerely,

Kathleen

KF/shp

Kathleen Fitzpatrick
Personal Manager

P.S. The enclosed is for your information. Dr. Peck is not affiliated with Forewords.

Bliss Road • New Preston • Connecticut • 06777 • 203-868-7400

Hugh Sidey

Writer

Writer for *Time* magazine. Author of *John F. Kennedy, President* and *A Very Personal Presidency: Lyndon Johnson.*

My all-time
most important book
was "The Discoverers" by
Dan Boorstin

Anne McCaffrey

Writer

Author of *Damia's Children*, *The Dolphins of Pern*, and *The City Who Fought*.

DRAGONHOLD - UNDERHILL

Timmore Lane, Newcastle County Wicklow, IRELAND
+353-1-2819936 (VOICE)   *+353-1-2810363 (F*

21 November 1994

Dear Kevin Kelly,

You've a foine brand of flattery there, m'laddie buck. As if my choice of books is going to incite more kids to read... Still, it's nice to be considered influential.   However, since you were kind enough to ask, I'll reply. My choices are entirely personal, and from my own preferred list - books that I myself have read and often reread for the sheer pleasure of the writing and the story, even when I know it so well I could probably recite passages by rote.

The book that had the most influence on me as a young woman (I was fourteen when I first encountered it) was Austin Tappan Wright's ISLANDIA.   This book gave me a personal philosophy which I have found both sustaining and stimulating. I reread it about every other year and I'm due for another reading soon.   KIM by Rudyard Kipling has been my long time top favorite and sort of a talisman in my family for my mother, my father and both my brothers always kept a copy of it to hand.   Of all the Geogette Heyer, and I find her equally as fine a story-teller as Kipling, I think the one that I enjoyed the most was THE UNKNOWN AJAX, a sort of high point for all her marvelous tales. KING HEREAFTER by Dorothy Dunnett is another of my rereads...the criterion for these being that, although I can remember scenes and whole passages, I still HAVE to reread them to recapture their special flavor and color.   DEEP WIZARDRY by Diane Duane is another I can reread with pleasure. THE BLUE SWORD by Robin McKinley also lives on the Special Shelf as does ONCE AND FUTURE KING by T. S White. Admittedly none of these are so-called Lit'rature but I have enjoyed them so much I always recommend them to others. THE HEALER'S WAR by Elizabeth Ann Scarborough is one of the most moving modern novels I've ever read.   A CASE OF CONSCIENCE by James Blish and that's it for me - only nine, I know, but mine own selection.

I haven't yet read the Greatest Book. I hope that I will one day find one that I could give such laurels.

Good luck on your project.   It's a worthy one.

Yours sincerely,

Anne McCaffrey BA SFWA Authors Guild, Ninc

Dave Barry

Writer/Humorist

Author of *Dave Barry Is Not Making This Up*, *Dave Barry Slept Here*, and *Dave Barry Does Japan*.

This is not exactly 10, but...

Everything by Robert Benchley
Everything by P.G. Wodehouse
All the Pogo books (by Walt Kelly)
Various dirty books I discovered when I was 13

November 23, 1994

Dear Kevin Kelly,

 I would go so far as to say that the person who has not digested
and appreciated the following books is a person who cannot possibly
understand themselves or the world surrounding them; a person who,
no matter how intelligent, can never be wise.

1. UNDERSTANDING MEDIA by Marshall McLuhan

2. THE TAO OF PHYSICS by Fritjof Capra

3. FOOD OF THE GODS by Terence McKenna

4. THE BOOK (ON THE TABOO AGAINST KNOWING WHO YOU ARE) by Alan Watts

5. SEX AND DRUGS by Robert Anton Wilson

6. THE POWER OF MYTH by Joseph Campbell

7. Any collection of essays by Gore Vidal

8. NEWS OF THE UNIVERSE by Robert Bly

9. ON GLORY ROADS by Eleanor Munro

10. SKINNY LEGS AND ALL by Tom Robbins

 As for the greatest book I ever read, I suppose it would be a three-
way tie between HUCKLEBERRRY FINN (Mark Twain), FINNEGANS WAKE
(James Joyce) and THE ARCHAIC REVIVAL (Terence McKenna). If one
could combine those three tomes, throw in a little Shakespeare,
a few panels of Krazy Kat, and a page or two from Henry Miller,
one would have the ultimate reading experience.

Good Luck,

Tom Robbins

Tom Robbins

Writer

Author of *Even Cowgirls Get the Blues, Half Asleep in Frog Pajamas,* and *Still Life with Woodpecker.*

Dear Kevin,

Your request is difficult to respond to. It can be interpreted in too many ways and there are just too many choices!

So as not to disappoint you, I am selecting the following off the top of my head...

The Bible
The Odyssey
Lao Tzu, The Way of Life
Sorokin, Ways and Power of Love
Schweitzer, Pilgrimage to Humanity
May, Man's Search for Himself
Jung, Memories, Dreams and Reflections
Fromm, The Art of Loving
Gandhi, Autobiography, The Story of My Experiments
                          with Truth
Dante, Inferno, Purgatorio, Paradiso

It is impossible for me to determine "the greatest book I have ever read."

I wish you well.

Warmly, *Leo Buscaglia*

Leo Buscaglia

Writer

Author of *Born for Love: Reflections on Loving, Bus 9 to Paradise*, and *Love*.

3rd July 1991.

Dear Mr. Kelly,

Thank you so much for your letter.

The books I think a well-read and well-educated person should read are those by our greatest historian Sir Arthur Bryant, who is now, sadly, dead.

They are:

The Age of Elegance
The Years of Endurance
The Years of Victory
The English Saga
The Fire and the Rose
The Years of Peril
Set in a Silver Sea.

They are all history books, and I would also say those by Christopher Hibbert, entitled:

George IV, Prince of Wales.
George IV, Regent and King.
The Virgin Queen
Captain Gronow.

These are history at its most accurate, most amusing and most delightful.

The greatest book I have ever read is 'The Bible'.

With all best wishes for your project.

Barbara Cartland

Writer

Author of *Bride to the King*, *Elizabethan Lover*, and *The Island of Love*.

                                        May 12, 1994

Dear Mr. Kelly:

    Your recent letter to Dr. Peale has come to
my attention. Dr. Peale passed away the afternoon
of December 24, 1993, in Pawling, New York. He
was 95 years of age.

    Since Dr. Peale was asked many times what
were the most important books to him, I am able to
answer your question: <u>The Holy Bible</u>, <u>The
Meditations of Marcus Aurelius</u>, <u>The Writings of
Ralph Waldo Emerson</u>, <u>The Autobiography of Benjamin
Franklin</u>, <u>The Life of Abraham Lincoln</u>, <u>I Dare You</u>
by William Danforth, <u>How to Win Friends and
Influence People</u> by Dale Carnegie, <u>Success Systems
that Never Fail</u> by W. Clement Stone, <u>Success
Through a Positive Mental Attitude</u> by Stone and
Napoleon Hill.

    With best wishes for success in your book
manuscript endeavor, I am

                          Cordially yours,

                          (Miss) Sybil Light
                          Secretary to Mrs. Peale

Norman V. Peale

Writer

Author of *The Power of Positive Thinking*, *The Power of
Positive Living*, and *How to Be Your Best*.

25 May 1991

Dear Mr. Kelly,

A hard quesion. My personal library numbers about 15,000 books, and in my three antiquarian and rare book shops I have an exteneded family of about 150,000 more, most of which I've at least upended.

I've read no fiction for many years, and probably the great 19th Century novels probably influenced me most. I don't like to read plays, which means I omit Shakespeare. I can't read Greek, Latin, Russian, Italian, or German, which make the true judgement hard in all those literatures also. Because influence is a matter of timing, after a certain age, with a certain amount of work behind one, one is almost un-influencable. My whole American generation was influenced, that is, jump-started by *On the Road*. But who speaks of Kerouac now?

My favorite novels are Don Quixote, War and Peace, Anna Karenina, Middlemarch. Yet three travel books, Kennan's Tent Life in Siberia, Wilfred Thesiger's Arabian Sands, and Eric Newsbys Slowly Down the Ganges are books I reread almost annually.

I cannot say what one book most influenced me most - On the Road, Hardy's The Woodlanders, and Yeats Collected Poems are candidates.

Best

[signature]

Larry McMurtry

Writer

Author of *Lonesome Dove* and *The Last Picture Show*.

Dear KEVIN KELLY, Thanks for your note. On the verge of a mier forever, I guess The MAGIC MOUNTAIN, first read in 1937, is my favorite of all these favorites.

1. Thomas MANN. The MAGIC MOUNTAIN
2. DANTE. la ~~Divine~~ COMMEDIA.
3. PROUST. à la Recherche du TEMPS PERDU.
4. MONTAIGNE, ESSAIS.
5. HAMLET. LEAR, RII. TEMPEST.
6. Lewis CARROLL, The HUNTING of the SNARK.
7. DICK FRANCIS, BANKER, The EDGE.
8. WORDSWORTH, The PRELUDE.
9. KAFKA, The TRIAL.
10. DOSTOEVSKI, NOTES from UNDERGROUND

Howard Lemerov,
25 vi 91

Howard Lemerov

Poet

Former Poet Laureat of the United States.

"We shouldn't teach great books;

we should teach a love of reading."

B. F. Skinner, quoted in Richard I. Evans,
B. F. Skinner: The Man and His Ideas

EDUCATORS

Ronald Mellor

Professor

Department Chair of History at University of
California, Los Angeles.

UNIVERSITY OF CALIFORNIA, LOS ANGELES

UCLA

BERKELEY • DAVIS • IRVINE • LOS ANGELES • RIVERSIDE • SAN DIEGO • SAN FRANCISCO

SANTA BARBARA • SANTA CRUZ

RONALD MELLOR
Chair
(310) 825-1883 Phone / (310) 206-9630 Fax
mellor@histr.sscnet.ucla.edu

DEPARTMENT OF HISTORY
405 HILGARD AVENUE
LOS ANGELES, CALIFORNIA 90024-1473

February 10, 1994

Dear Mr. Kelly:

Thank you for your letter requesting a list of books, which I feel a well read person should
have read. Since I was trained as a classicist in the old days, when I studied Latin and
Greek--even in High School in New York, I naturally look to classical text as paradigms.
My own preferences are Homer's "Odyssey" (I like the "Iliad" much less), "The Tragedies
of Euripides", the philosophical writings of Plato, who was able to make philosophy into a
living dramatic story and among the Romans, I'm afraid I have to say the historian,
Tacitus--I'm afraid because I have just had a book published on Tacitus. Perhaps I should
be guilty in skipping over other ancient writers, but I would like to include Shakespeare,
Dostoyovski's "Crime and Punishment", at least something of Dickens and something of
Jane Austin, for a woman's perspective on the early 18th century. I think my personal
favorite is "Pride and Prejudice" or "Emma". In our own century, I am not sure that one
can say that there are books that any well read person should have read, in quite the same
way. I enjoyed Guntegras' "The Tin Drum", Ignacio Silone's "Bread and Wine", or Andre
Malraux's "Man's Fate". I noticed that they are all novels in which individual emotions are
painted against a strongly historical framework. In mentioning works of history, perhaps
the greatest of all histories written in English should be included, even if it does happen to
be on my own field, Roman History. That is the marvelous Edward Gibbon's "Decline and
Fall of the Roman Empire". Not many people have read all 3,000 pages, but reading at
least a few chapters ought to be a requirement of being literate in the English language. I
think that the greatest literary material that I have or better, seen, is Shakespeare. Both
the comedies and the tragedies. Although, I think that something truly is lost, by simply
reading them on the page. This was a man of the theatre, in fact, he was an actor who has
made his name better known to those who speak English, than any political leader, king,
prime minister, general or admiral in the history English speaking peoples. It is
remarkable that those plays can be staged now, 400 years later, in modern dress, in all
sorts of ways, in numerous languages and they still have a remarkable power, the almost
universal power of a Hamlet or a King Lear.

Sincerely,

Ronald J. Mellor
Chair

9 Nov. 1990

Dear Mr. Kelly,

Probably the book I most enjoyed was Joseph Conrad's <u>Nostromo</u>, which I read in very favorable circumstances. The writer who has meant most to me is Wordsworth. The books I think people should read are Plato, Shakespeare, <u>War and Peace</u>, Rousseau's <u>Confessions</u> and other works by him, <u>The Norton Anthology of Poetry</u>, Proust, Brecht, and various works of Hegel.

Sincerely,

David Perkins
Marquand Professor of
English Literature

Marquand Professor of English Literature at Harvard University

David Perkins

Professor

Marquand Professor of English Literature at Harvard University.

Dear Mr. Kelly:

Here are some books as they come to mind (I'll stop when I get to twenty!):

Homer, Iliad
Sophocles, Oedipus the King
Plato, Symposium
Augustine, Confessions
Dante, Divine Comedy
King James Bible
works of Shakespeare
Milton, Paradise Lost
Boswell, Life of Samuel Johnson
Wordsworth, poems
Dickens, Great Expectations
George Eliot, Middlemarch
Joyce, Ulysses
Freud, Civilization and Its Discontents
Freud, Beyond the Pleasure Principle
Huizinga, Home Ludens
Weber, The Protestant Ethic and the Spirit of Capitalism
Communist Manifesto
Weinberg, The First Three Minutes.

As for the greatest book I ever read, that would depend on "greatest" in some particular respect. The book that's most important for me in my profession (teaching English literature) is the Bible; the book that's most intellectually interesting to me right now is Weinberg's on modern cosmology; the book that maybe had the greatesty emotional impact on me when I read it was Joyce's Ulysses.

Sincerely yours,

Darrel Mansell

Darrel Mansel

Professor

English Professor at Dartmouth College.

Noel Perrin

Professor

Professor of English at Dartmouth College.

Dartmouth College HANOVER • NEW HAMPSHIRE • 03755

Department of English, Sanborn House • TELEPHONE: (603) 646-2316

4 Nov. 90

Dear Mr. Kelly,

There is no one greatest book
I have ever read. <u>Moby-Dick</u>, <u>Paradise Lost</u>,
<u>War & Peace</u>, <u>The Lord of the Rings</u> would be
among the greatest.

As to a list of 10-20, you'll find one
in a book of mine called <u>A Reader's Delight</u>.

Sincerely,

Noel Perrin

Noel Perrin

Phil Shaver

Professor

Professor in Psychology at University of California, Davis.

1/30/94

The books that have had a lasting effect on me are ones related to my field, psychology:

Freud, *The Interpretation of Dreams*.

Freud + Breuer, *Studies in Hysteria*.

Darwin, *Origin of Species*.

Darwin, *Expression of Emotions in Animals and Man*.

William James, *Principles of Psychology*.

"   ", *Varieties of Religious Experience*.

Marvin Harris, *Cows, Pigs, Wars, and Witches: The Riddles of Culture*.

John Bowlby, *Attachment and Loss*, Vols. I, II, III.

— Phil Shaver

I also like poetry, especially Adrienne Rich, *The Dream of a Common Language*.

Mrs Vendler:

I am an English major at San Diego State University and working on a book about what knowledgeable and successful people read. If it is possible, I would like a list of ten to twenty books that you feel a well read and well educated person should read or simply should have read. Also, I would like to know what you feel is the greatest book you have ever read (it doesn't have to be on your initial list). This would be greatly appreciated. Thank you for your time.

A list for Americans :

Sincerely,

Kevin H. Kelly

The Bible : Genesis, Job, Luke
Plato : Apology + Crito
Sophocles : Oedipus Rex
Cervantes : Don Quixote (abridged)
Shakespeare : Hamlet ; King Lear   Dickens : Great Expectations
E. Brontë : Wuthering Heights
Whitman : Song of Myself + other poems from Leaves of Grass .
Dostoevsky : Crime and Punishment ; A. Chekhov : Stories
Lincoln : Gettysburg address + Inaugural Addresses
Faulkner : Any one of the great novels : Absalom, Absalom or The Sound + the Fury

Yours,
H. Vendler

Helen Vendler

Professor

Professor of English and American Literature at Harvard University.

DEPARTMENT OF PHILOSOPHY
BRIGHAM YOUNG UNIVERSITY
3196 JESSE KNIGHT HUMANITIES BUILDING
PO BOX 26279
PROVO, UTAH 84602-6279
(801) 378-2721

February 4, 1994

Here are some books that I think would help a Western person be well-read. I don't have any idea how to list the books *everyone* should have read. I don't mean to be rude, but I'm not confident there is such a list since education is not a matter of gathering facts or reading the right books.

To be honest, I don't really see the point of putting together this list, though I'll give you the benefit of the doubt and send along my suggestions. Obviously, the list would be different for Japanese or Chinese or Indian or African people. In addition, what's so important about the number ten? Why not "nine books everyone should have read" or twelve or twenty-three? And why books rather than poems or plays or essays?

> Bible
> Shakespeare's plays and sonnets
> Augustine, *Confessions*
> Nietzsche, *Genealogy of Morals*
> Plato, *Symposium*
> Aristotle, *Nichomachean Ethics*
> Rilke, *Sonnets to Orpheus* or *Duino Elegies*
> Hölderlin, "The Rhine," "Patmos," or "Mnemosyne"
> Marx, *Capital*
> Darwin, *Origin of Species*

I've not listed these in any particular order except that in which they came to mind.

The most influential book I've read is the Book of Mormon.

Sincerely,

James E. Faulconer
Chair

James E. Faulconer

Professor

Professor of Philosophy at Brigham Young University.

UNIVERSITY OF CALIFORNIA, SANTA CRUZ

BERKELEY • DAVIS • IRVINE • LOS ANGELES • RIVERSIDE • SAN DIEGO • SAN FRANCISCO   SANTA BARBARA • SANTA CRUZ

BOARD OF STUDIES IN LITERATURE   March 9, 1994
                                        SANTA CRUZ, CALIFORNIA 95064

Dear Mr. Kelly:

The books I suggest are as follows:

1. The whole <u>Bible</u>

2. N. Chomsky <u>Syntactic Structures</u>

3. Homer <u>The Iliad</u>

4. Homer <u>The Odyssey</u>

5. Chaucer <u>The Canterbury Tales</u>

6. Thomas <u>Calculus & Analytic Geometry</u>

7. Darwin <u>The Origin of Species</u>

8. <u>The Thousand and One Nights</u>

9. Russel & Whitehead <u>Principia Mathematica</u>

10. <u>The Koran</u>

Sincerely,

Jorge Hankamer

Jorge Hankamer
Chair, Literature Board

Jorge Hankamer

Professor

Chair of the Literature Board of University of California, Santa Cruz.

Dartmouth College HANOVER · NEW HAMPSHIRE · 03755-3533

Department of English, 6032 Sanborn House · TELEPHONE: (603) 646-2316

Dear Kevin Kelly:

You ask an impossible question, but for all that, here's my response.

Ten Literary Works for the Well-Read Person

Paradise Lost (entire), John Milton
One of the following writers' collected poems: William Words-
    worth, Emily Dickinson, Wallace Stevens
Fear and Trembling, S. Kierkegaard
Book equivalent: "Bartleby the Scrivener" (story), Herman Mel-
    ville, and "Song of Myself" (poem), Walt Whitman
Crime and Punishment, Dostoyevsky
Jane Eyre, C. Bronte
The Interpretation of Dreams, Sigmund Freud
A Portrait of the Artist as a Young Man, James Joyce
Swann's Way, Marcel Proust
One Hundred Years of Solitude, Gabriel Marquez

The greatest book I ever read? probably Marcel Proust's A La
    Recherche du Temps Perdu, complete.

Sincerely,

Louis A. Renza, Chair
Department of English
Dartmouth College

Louis A. Renza

Professor

Department of English Chair at Dartmouth College.

If you love to read, there is always the
fear that you may have missed an important book, the one that could explain the
workings of the world and all the mysteries
of life, too.

I read for knowledge, inspiration, ideas,
solace, enjoyment--and much, much more.
Best of all, though, is the thrill of
recognition when something I've just read
brings together threads from many sources
and weaves them into a new tapestry...or
gives me new insights and understanding
of something I've known all my life.
Therein lies the adventure!

Wishing you every success,

Warmest regards,

Nancy Landon Kassebaum
United States Senator

6

POLITICIANS

George Bush

Politician

Former President of the United States of America.

GEORGE BUSH

February 3, 1995

Dear Kevin:

"Books," wrote Henry David Thoreau, "are the treasured wealth of the world and the fit inheritance of generations and nations." How right he was.

Reading is one of Barbara's and my greatest joys. We both read a lot as youngsters and still try to keep up with new releases. One of my favorites as a child was *Treasure Island*, and I recently read and thoroughly enjoyed *D-Day* by Stephen Ambrose.

Reading enables us to enjoy the rewards of lifelong learning, and your library is a vibrant center of learning -- use it!

With best wishes,

Sincerely,

G Bush

Dan Quayle

Politician

Former Vice-President of the United States of America.

THE VICE PRESIDENT
WASHINGTON

November 26, 1990

Dear Kevin:

Thank you very much for taking time out of your day to send me a letter. You write very well, and it was good to hear from you.

I enjoy reading a variety of books, but my favorites are history books. It is interesting to learn about the events and circumstances which have brought us to where we are today. I also enjoyed <u>Robinson Crusoe</u>.

I am glad to know that you also take such an interest in reading. It continues to be one of my favorite hobbies.

Thank you again for your letter. Keep up the good work!

Sincerely,

Dan Quayle

Paul Simon

Politician

Senator of Illinois, Democrat

PAUL SIMON
ILLINOIS

United States Senate
WASHINGTON, DC 20510–1302

April 16, 1991

Dear Kevin:

I apologize for the delay in getting back to you and your request for a suggested reading list.

I really can't say what others should read because everyone has different tastes. But I can give you a list of my favorite books.

They include:
"Black Boy" by Richard Wright
"Abraham Lincoln" by Benjamin Platt Thomas
"The Making of the President -- 1960" by Theodore H. White
"The Echo of Greece" by Edith Hamilton
"I'd Do It Again" by James Michael Curley
"Working" by Studs Terkel
"The Guns of August" by Barbara Tuchman
"The Search of History: A Personal Adventure" by Theodore H. White
"The Autobiography of William Allen White" by William Allen White
The Bible

The book that really moved me when I was 12 years old was "Black Boy." My parents had been active in civil rights matters, but not until I read that book did the awesomeness of racial prejudice hit me.

I hope you find this helpful. Thank you for your interest and good luck with your book.

Cordially,

Paul Simon
U.S. Senator

PS/ph

230 S. DEARBORN
KLUCZYNSKI BLDG., 38TH FLOOR
CHICAGO, IL 60604
312/353-4952

3 WEST OLD CAPITOL PLAZA
SUITE 1
SPRINGFIELD, IL 62701
217/492-4960

8787 STATE ST.
SUITE 212
EAST ST. LOUIS, IL 62203
618/398-7707

250 WEST CHERRY
ROOM 115-B
CARBONDALE, IL 62901
618/457-3653

Lamar Alexander

Politician

Former Governor of Tennessee and the former Secretary of
Education. Candidate for the 1996 Presidential Election.

BAKER, WORTHINGTON, CROSSLEY, STANSBERRY & WOOLF

ATTORNEYS AT LAW
1700 NASHVILLE CITY CENTER
POST OFFICE BOX 190613
NASHVILLE, TENNESSEE 37219

TELEPHONE 615 726-5600
TELECOPIER 615 726-5739

WASHINGTON, D.C.
KNOXVILLE, TENNESSEE
HUNTSVILLE, TENNESSEE
JOHNSON CITY, TENNESSEE
HENDERSONVILLE, TENNESSEE

LAMAR ALEXANDER

February 18, 1994

Dear Kevin,

Thanks for writing to request a list of my favorite books. I've enclosed my reading list that was printed in last December's *American Spectator*. I'd also add anything written by Dave Barry and Roy Blount, Jr., whom I think are two of the funniest writers today.

Very best wishes.

Sincerely,

Lamar Alexander

All the King's Men, by Robert Penn Warren. For the person who gets to thinking he or she knows something about politics or about writing, this will bring you down to earth.

Abraham Lincoln: A Biography, by Benjamin P. Thomas. "In 268 words he gave us a chart and a compass . . . demonstrating that our nation's strength lies in rededication to those beliefs to which it was committed at birth." Timely advice. The best short biography of Lincoln.

The Discoverers, by Daniel Boorstin. For mold-breakers. When I was governor, trying to make schools better, I read a chapter each night. "The enemy of discovery is the profession." Boorstin is the best teacher today of the idea of America.

A Death in the Family, by James Agee. Just about the best writing you can ever find about what it is like to sit on a porch in the warm evenings laughing and smelling the hoses spraying the lawn and watching the children put fireflies in jars. Just about the best writing, period.

Pat Nixon: The Untold Story, by Julie Nixon Eisenhower. Especially for Nixon fans (I am one), especially this year. "Oh, no thank you, Judy, I have to do things for myself. I tell my girls that if you become dependent on others and let them do everything for you, you become ugly."

Bridge to the Sun, by Gwen Terasaki. A Tennessee girl falls in love with a Japanese diplomat just before Pearl Harbor, marries him, is deported, and lives in the mountains of Japan during World War II.

Six Months Off: An American Family's Australian Adventure, by Lamar Alexander. I like to read it because it is about our family.

Crackers, by Roy Blount, Jr. About the Carters, but it could be the Clintons: "I've got the red neck White House blues/Jimmy's (Billy's) got me all confused/He's in all the right churches and all the wrong pews/I've got the red neck White House blues."

Roots, by Alex Haley. Admit it. You've watched it but never read it. See if you don't sit up straight when slave traders snatch Kunta Kinte from the canebrake. Every family's struggle for freedom.

Alexander and the Terrible, Horrible, No Good, Very Bad Day, by Judith Viorst. Bedtime reading. For your grandchild, your legislator, or yourself. We all have these days—often during holidays: "I think I'll move to Australia."

Dear Mr. Kelly:

Your question regarding reading materials was interesting to contemplate, and probably my response would differ on a day-to-day basis. Today my list of ten books that would seem most valuable and helpful to a unsullied reader would include:

1. MOBY DICK by Herman Melville
2. THE ILIAD by Homer
3. TALE OF TWO CITIES by Charles Dickens
4. The Collected Works of William Shakespeare
5. HISTORY OF THE WORLD by Arnold Spengler
6. THE ART OF WAR by Sun Tzu
7. THE STRANGER by Albert Camus
8. THE BROTHERS KARAMAZOV by Feodor Dostoevsky
9. FOR WHOM THE BELL TOLLS by Ernest Hemingway
10. ON THE ROAD by Jack Kerouac

I would also include THE BIBLE as a compilation of Christian Scriptures, and other spiritual statements as representative of the religions of the world.

Best of luck on your project.

With best regards, I am

Very truly yours,

Mike Sullivan
Governor

P.S. I do not "do" fan mail.

MS: ib

Mike Sullivan

Politician

Governor of Wyoming.

Edward T. Schafer

Politician

Governor of North Dakota.

**EDWARD T. SCHAFER
GOVERNOR**

State of North Dakota

OFFICE OF THE GOVERNOR
600 E. Boulevard - Ground Floor
BISMARCK, NORTH DAKOTA 58505-0001
(701) 224-2200

June 16, 1994

Dear Kevin,

Thank you for contacting my office with your request. I appreciate your interest in my position as Governor.

The following is a list of books that a well-read, well-educated person should read:

Atlas Shrugged, by Ayn Rand
Grapes of Wrath, by John Steinbeck
The History of the World, by H.G. Wells
Arms and The Man, by Bernard Shaw
To Kill a Mockingbird, by Harper Lee
Beyond the Bedroom Wall, by Larry Woiwode
The Fields, The Trees, The Town, by Conrad Richter
Ranch Life and the Hunting Trail, by Theodore Roosevelt
The Bible
Divine Comedy, by Dante

The greatest book I have read is The History of the World.

Best wishes with your project!

Sincerely,

Edward T. Schafer
Governor

13:17:06

Michael Manley

Politician

Prime Minister of Jamaica.

Office of the Prime Minister

Jamaica House
Kingston

October 3, 1991.

Dear Mr. Kelly,

      I got your letter about books that might have influenced me.

      Dostoevsky's "The Brothers Karamazov" influenced me particularly because of the tremendous section questioning the very concept of God because of the evil which occurs in the world.   The contradiction which prompts the discussion is not new but presented with incredible force.

      "The Idiot" by the same author made a profound impression on me when I was young because of the subtlety with which it explores female psychology on the one hand, and the ambivalence which is provoked by Prince Myshkin's saintly simplicity.

      Tolstoy's "War and Peace" struck me most forcibly because of its examination of the role of chance in the unfolding of history.

      Hegel influenced me profoundly because he provided an analytical framework within which to understand history.   I have had a belief in dialectics ever since.

      I continue to think Karl Marx one of the most important historians in modern civilisation.   I regret that his idealistic hopes ending with the withering away of the State will not be realised.   That prospect is itself a victim of too many contradictions.

      Harold Laski's "Grammar of Politics" and "Reflections on the Revolution of our Time" did much to sharpen my contemporary political sensibilities.

      Thomas Mann's "Magic Mountain" influenced me by provoking an awareness of the history of ideas quite beyond what the normal pedagogic procedures had been able to induce.

      These books spring to mind at the moment though I have no doubt if I was not under a certain amount of pressure, others would probably occur to me.

      As to the greatest book, this is an almost impossible question. I think it would be true to say that the book that gripped me the most, perhaps because I found its inner resonances so subtle and so reflective of the human condition, was "The Idiot".

    Good luck with your project.

          Yours sincerely,

          Michael Manley

David Duke

Politician

Ran for Governor of Louisiana in 1992.

David Duke

500 N. Arnoult Rd. Metairie, LA 70001

February 10th, 1994

Dear Mr. Kelly:

Thanks **very** much for your recent letter. I appreciate your questions and the opportunity to clarify my position(s).

You asked for a list of books I feel a well-read, well-educated person should have in his/her collection. I'll tell you some of my own favorite titles. As a history major (B.A., LSU, 1974), you might expect that most of them deal in history and politics.

1. *The Dispossessed Majority*   by Wilmot Robertson
2. *Conscience of a Conservative*   Sen. Barry Goldwater
3. *Decline & Fall of the Roman Empire*   Edward Gibbon
4. The Holy Bible
5. *The Origin of Races*   Carleton Coon
6. *Democracy in America*   Alexis deToqueville
7. *The Origin of Species*   Charles Darwin
8. *Hereditary Genius*   Sir Francis Galton
9. *Paved with Good Intentions*   S. Jared Taylor
10. *Nineteen Eighty-Four*   George Orwell

Kevin, it's tough to choose only ten. A few that were hard to leave out of the top ten: *"Race"* by Dr. John R. Baker, *"Right from the Beginning"* by Pat Buchanan, *"Which Way Western Man"* by W. G. Simpson, *"The Federalist Papers"* by John Jay, *"Race and Reality"* by Carleton Putnam, and *"The Count of Monte Cristo"* by Alexandre Dumas.

I hope this list is helpful to you. Best of luck in all endeavors.

Respectfully,

David Duke

Ed Koch

Politician

Former Mayor of New York City.

ROBINSON SILVERMAN PEARCE ARONSOHN & BERMAN

1290 AVENUE OF THE AMERICAS

NEW YORK, NEW YORK 10104

(212) 541-2000

FACSIMILE:(212) 541-4630

WRITER'S DIRECT NUMBER:

(212) 541-2100

FLORIDA OFFICE:
520 BRICKELL KEY DRIVE
MIAMI, FLORIDA 33131
(305) 374-3800
FACSIMILE: (305) 374-1156

May 10, 1994

Dear Mr. Kelly:

I have your letter. I prefer not to provide a list of books that I propose others read because I have read them. None of the books I have read over the years to the best of my knowledge affected my career in the private sector or in the public sector. To indicate otherwise by listing a set of books would be pretentious.

All the best.

Sincerely,

Edward I. Koch

Hazel O'Leary

Politician

The Secretary of Energy during Clinton's presidency.

Department of Energy
Washington, DC 20585

August 9, 1994

Dear Mr. Kelly:

On behalf of Secretary of Energy Hazel R. O'Leary, we appreciate your letter inquiring about a list of books that knowledgeable and successful people should read.

Enclosed are a list of books that were found in the Secretary's personal bookcase in her office. The books include, <u>The Seven Habits of Highly Effective People</u> by Stephen Covey, <u>Principle Centered Leadership</u> by Stephen Covey, <u>The Agenda</u> by Bob Woodward, <u>The Career Makers</u> by John Sibbald, <u>Let's Talk Quality</u> by Philip Crosby, <u>The Real World Order</u> by Singer & Wildavsky, and <u>Shattered Peace</u> by Daniel Yergin.

We strongly believe reading is very important, and fear that children are opting to get their information visually rather than through reading.

Your interest is greatly appreciated. Good luck in your future endeavors.

Sincerely,

Barbara Semedo

Barbara Semedo
Press Secretary
Office of Public and
Consumer Affairs

Thomas P. O'Neill, Jr.
Room 1008
Thomas P. O'Neill, Jr. Federal Building
10 Causeway Street
Boston, Massachusetts 02222

Speaker
U.S. House of Representatives
1977-1986

Telephone No. (617) 720-4000

Member of Congress
8th District, Massachusetts
1953-1986

July 9, 1991

Dear Kevin:

Thank you for writing me requesting a list of books that influenced me the most. A few that come to mind are the following:

The Outer Most House by Betson
The Power Game by Smith
Iacocca by Lee Iacocca
Trinity by Leon Uris
Profiles in Courage by JFK
Mortal Friends by Jim Carroll

I trust this will be satisfactory.

With every good wish,

Sincerely,

Thomas P. O'Neill, Jr.

"Tip" O'Neill

Politician

Former Speaker of the House.

HENRY G. CISNEROS

March 18, 1995

Dear Mr. Kelly:

Thank you for your recent letter expressing interest in a list of books that I recommend as good reading material.

The following is a list of books that I recommend:

	Title		Author
1)	Lincoln at Gettysburg	-	Garry Wills
2)	Meditations	-	Marcus Aurelius
3)	Leadership	-	James MacGregor Burns
4)	The Republic	-	Plato
5)	Imitation of Christ	-	Thomas A. Kempis
6)	Miracle at Philadelphia-- The Constitution	-	Catherine D. Bowen
7)	Roosevelt Lion and the Fox (Biography of President Franklin Roosevelt)	-	James MacGregor Burns
9)	The Killer Angels	-	Michael Shaara

In addition, the greatest book I have read is the Bible.

I agree that reading is important and wish you much success in your project.

Sincerely,

Henry G. Cisneros

Henry G. Cisneros

Howell Heflin

Polititian

Senator of Alabama, Democrat.

HOWELL HEFLIN
ALABAMA

COMMITTEE ON AGRICULTURE,
NUTRITION, AND FORESTRY
COMMITTEE ON ENERGY AND
NATURAL RESOURCES
COMMITTEE ON THE JUDICIARY
SELECT COMMITTEE ON ETHICS

☐ 728 SENATE HART BUILDING
WASHINGTON, DC 20510-0101
(202) 224-4124

United States Senate

WASHINGTON, DC 20510-0101

STATE OFFICES:

☐ 355 FEDERAL BUILDING
1800 FIFTH AVENUE NORTH
BIRMINGHAM, AL 35203
(205) 731-1500

☐ 113 ST. JOSEPH STREET
437 U.S. COURTHOUSE
MOBILE, AL 36602
(205) 432-7715

☐ FEDERAL COURTHOUSE, B-29
15 LEE STREET
MONTGOMERY, AL 36104
(205) 265-9507

☐ 105 MAIN STREET
P.O. BOX 228
TUSCUMBIA, AL 35674
(205) 381-7060

April 15, 1991

Dear Mr. Kelly:

I am writing to acknowledge, with thanks, receipt of your recent inquiry with respect to a list of books I have read. It is my policy to refrain from listing what I believe are the ten best books or what I believe other people should read.

I consider the Bible the very best book that I have read, and I do read contemporary novels, biographies and history. I also read publications dealing with the judiciary and many magazines as I feel it is important to keep up on current events. My time is limited, therefore my in-depth reading of a subject is usually limited to the legislative issue I am currently working on.

With kindest regards, I am

Sincerely yours,

Howell Heflin

HH/bms

Ted Stevens

Politician

Senator of Alaska, Republican.

United States Senate

COMMITTEE ON APPROPRIATIONS
WASHINGTON, DC 20510–6025

July 11, 1994

Dear Mr. Kelly:

Thank you for your letter regarding your work on a book about what knowledgeable and successful people read. It is good to see people who want to encourage the education of children and adults through reading.

The books that were most influential to me are The Bible, Churchill's World War II series, The Count of Monte Cristo, The Iliad, The American Caesar, Death of a President, The Last Lion, parts I and II, and President Nixon's books: Beyond Peace; Seize the Moment: America's Challenge in a One-Superpower World; The Real War; 1999: Victory Without War; Leaders; Six Crises; In the Arena: A Memoir of Victory, Defeat, and Renewal; Real Peace: No More Vietnams; Real Peace: A Strategy for the West.

Thanks again for your letter and good luck on your book.

With best wishes,

Cordially,

TED STEVENS

John McCain

Politician

Senator of Arizona, Republican.

JOHN McCAIN
ARIZONA

COMMITTEE ON ARMED SERVICES
COMMITTEE ON COMMERCE, SCIENCE,
AND TRANSPORTATION
COMMITTEE ON GOVERNMENTAL AFFAIRS
COMMITTEE ON INDIAN AFFAIRS
SPECIAL COMMITTEE ON AGING

United States Senate

111 RUSSELL SENATE OFFICE BUILDING
WASHINGTON, DC 20510-0303
(202) 224-2235

1839 SOUTH ALMA SCHOOL ROAD
SUITE 375
MESA, AZ 85210
(602) 491-4300

2400 EAST ARIZONA
BILTMORE CIRCLE
SUITE 1150
PHOENIX, AZ 85016
(602) 952-2410

450 WEST PASEO REDONDO
SUITE 200
TUCSON, AZ 85701
(602) 670-6334

TELEPHONE FOR HEARING IMPAIRED
(202) 224-7132
(602) 952-0170

June 27, 1994

Dear Mr. Kelly:

Thank you for your letter regarding the importance of reading. I commend you for your opinion on reading and its importance to any educated person.

Reading helps our youth realize their goals and it is important that they are encouraged to take advantage of any reading opportunity available to them.

Following are some books that have most influenced my life:

- The Last Lion, Volume II
- For Whom The Bell Tolls
- The Influence of Seapower on History
- The Decline and Fall of The Roman Empire
- The Great Gatsby

I hope that this information will be useful and wish you luck on your future endeavors. Please feel free to contact my office if I can be of any further service.

Sincerely,

John McCain
United States Senator

JM/jcd

PRINTED ON RECYCLED PAPER

Sam Nunn

Politician

Senator of Georgia, Democrat.

SAM NUNN, GEORGIA, CHAIRMAN

J. JAMES EXON, NEBRASKA
CARL LEVIN, MICHIGAN
EDWARD M. KENNEDY, MASSACHUSETTS
JEFF BINGAMAN, NEW MEXICO
ALAN J. DIXON, ILLINOIS
JOHN GLENN, OHIO
ALBERT GORE, JR., TENNESSEE
TIMOTHY E. WIRTH, COLORADO
RICHARD C. SHELBY, ALABAMA
ROBERT C. BYRD, WEST VIRGINIA

JOHN W. WARNER, VIRGINIA
STROM THURMOND, SOUTH CAROLINA
WILLIAM S. COHEN, MAINE
PETE WILSON, CALIFORNIA
JOHN McCAIN, ARIZONA
MALCOLM WALLOP, WYOMING
SLADE GORTON, WASHINGTON
TRENT LOTT, MISSISSIPPI
DAN COATS, INDIANA

ARNOLD L. PUNARO, STAFF DIRECTOR
PATRICK A. TUCKER, STAFF DIRECTOR FOR THE MINORITY

United States Senate

COMMITTEE ON ARMED SERVICES
WASHINGTON, DC 20510–6050

April 16, 1991

Dear Mr. Kelly:

Thank you for your recent letter asking me about my favorite books. Although it is hard to select specific favorites, Victor Hugo's <u>Les Miserables</u> is among my favorites, as is Mark Twain's <u>Huckleberry Finn</u>. I also enjoy reading biographies and history. As Winston Churchill observed, "The farther backward you can look, the farther forward you can see."

Sincerely,

Sam Nunn

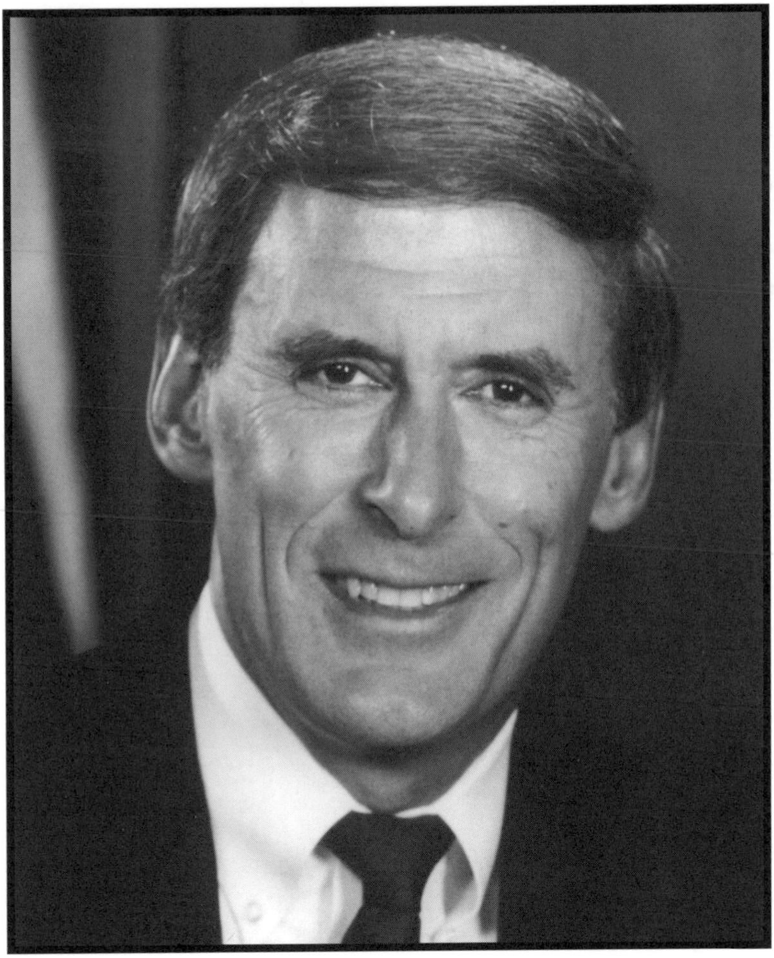

Dan Coats

Politician

Senator of Indiana, Republican.

DAN COATS
INDIANA

411 RUSSELL SENATE OFFICE BUILDING
(202) 224-5623

INDIANAPOLIS OFFICE:
ROOM 447, 46 EAST OHIO STREET
INDIANAPOLIS, INDIANA 46204
(317) 226-5555

COMMITTEES:
ARMED SERVICES
LABOR AND HUMAN
RESOURCES

United States Senate
WASHINGTON, DC 20510

11 January 1994

Dear Kevin:

Thank you for your letter of 10 January in re: a list of ten books
that you feel a well read and well educated person should read or
simply should have read.

My list would be as follows:

1) The Holy Bible
2) Shakespeare - Macbeth
3) Chaucer - The Canterbury Tales
4) Homer - The Iliad
5) Homer - The Odyssey
6) Milton - Paradise Lost
7) Dante - The Inferno
8) Hamilton, Jay, and Madison - The Federalist Papers
9) Twain - Huckelberry Finn, Tom Sawyer
10) Lincoln - Collected Works, Speeches and Writings

As for the book that I have most enjoyed: William Manchester's **The
Last Lion** and **Alone**.

Thank you again for your interest.

Sincerely yours,

Dan Coats
U.S. Senator
4)

Richard Lugar

Politician

Senator of Indiana, Republican.

RICHARD G. LUGAR
INDIANA

SH 306 SENATE OFFICE BUILDING
WASHINGTON, DC 20510
202-224-4814

COMMITTEES:

FOREIGN RELATIONS

AGRICULTURE, NUTRITION, AND FORESTRY

United States Senate

WASHINGTON, DC 20510-1401

March 21, 1991

Dear Mr. Kelly:

Thank you for your recent correspondence inquiring about my favorite book. Literacy is an important part of education and I greatly appreciate your interest and involvement in reading.

My favorite book is "Surprised By Joy" by C.S. Lewis. I have found this to be a wonderful and exciting personal story of religious discovery and conversion.

I strongly support literacy programs. I encourage you to continue your interest in reading as it contributes greatly to learning and education.

Thank you again for writing.

Sincerely,

Richard G. Lugar
United States Senator

RGL:ljl

William S. Cohen

Politician

Senator of Maine, Republican.

WILLIAM S. COHEN
MAINE

United States Senate

WASHINGTON, DC 20510–1901

SENATOR WILLIAM S. COHEN'S FAVORITE BOOKS ON AMERICAN HISTORY

The March of Folly Barbara Tuchman

The Vineyard of Liberty James MacGregor Burns

America Alistar Cooke

In Search of History Theodore White

The Essential Walter Lippmann

The Next American Frontier Robert Reich

The Nine Nations of North America Joel Garreau

The Third Wave Alvin Toffler

Future Shock Alvin Toffler

Megatrends John Naisbitt

Conrad Burns

Politician

Senator of Montana, Republican.

CONRAD BURNS
MONTANA

COMMITTEES:
COMMERCE, SCIENCE, AND
TRANSPORTATION
ENERGY AND NATURAL RESOURCES
SMALL BUSINESS

United States Senate
WASHINGTON, DC 20510-2603

May 9, 1991

Dear Kevin:

Thank you for your recent letter. It sounds as if your book will be an interesting one.

The greatest book I have ever read is <u>Last of the Lions</u> by Winston Churchill, and I would highly recommend putting this on your list. As for a list of ten books a well educated person should read, I would not even attempt to form a list. There are so many good books available, covering such a wide array of topics, it would be unfair to try to limit them to ten.

I hope you take advantage of the list you compile. I have no doubt that your education would be broadened by reading the books recommended to you. Good luck with your studies.

With best wishes,

Sincerely,

Conrad Burns
United States Senator

CRB/pad

Harry Reid

Politician

Senator of Nevada, Democrat.

To: Kevin H. Kelly

From: Senator Harry Reid

Re: Favorite Authors/Books

Date: June 27, 1994

1. Bible and Book of Mormon

2. Durant's eleven volumes of History of Civilization

3. *Rise and Fall of the Third Reich* by William Shirer

4. *Nicholas and Alexander* by Robert Massie

5. *Complete works of Emily Dickenson*

6. *Peter the Great* by Robert Massie

7. *The Last Lion* by William Manchester

8. *Exodus* by Leon Uris

9. Tony Hillerman (Anything he writes)

10. *The Call of the Wild* by Jack London

George Mitchell

Politician

Senator of Maine, Democrat.

GEORGE J. MITCHELL
MAINE

United States Senate
WASHINGTON, DC 20510–1902

April 23, 1991

Dear Mr. Kelly:

Thank you for your recent letter asking what I perceive to be ten influential books. I appreciate hearing from you.

As I am sure you are well aware, the time constraints imposed on me by my duties as Majority Leader prohibit a lengthy discourse on this issue. I will however attempt to provide a brief explanation in my choice of each work. I have included works which have been influential to me as well as those which I believe would benefit others. They do not appear in any particular order.

Given the impact they have had on several civilizations and countless generations, I would begin with the Bible and the Koran. Both have been, and continue to be, influential and our understanding and appreciation of these books may enhance our ability to relate to the people whose ideologies they represent.

I believe the study of history is also an integral part of this brief sample in understanding our own society. For this category I have chosen three works. The History of the Decline and Fall of the Roman Empire by Sir Edward Gibbon is one of the most comprehensive works about that civilization. A Distant Mirror: The Calamitous 14th Century is by Barbara Tuchman who gained unique recognition for her works and was one of the foremost historians of our century. The third work in this category is the Rise and Fall of the Great Powers written by Paul Kennedy only a few years ago and is another insightful reflection on the evolution of civilizations.

Kevin Kelly
April 23, 1991
Page 2

These works are indeed a mirror of our own era, all of which
have faced its share of economic booms and battles, diseases
and despots.

Regarding literature I would include the <u>Iliad</u> and <u>Odyssey</u>
by Homer and the <u>Complete Works of William Shakespeare</u>,
neither of which require lengthy justifications for their
inclusion in this list. I also add <u>Arundel</u> or other works by
Kenneth Roberts in the category of children's literature. As
you know, I represent the state of Maine. Roberts' works of
historical fiction transpire in colonial Maine. They are rich
in descriptive narrative and are a wonderful source for
personal enrichment of young minds.

As a student at Bowdoin College and, later, as a law
student at Georgetown, I was immersed in courses focusing on
logic and reasoning. As such, I submit for this list one of
the greatest philosophical treatises, <u>The Summa Theologiae</u> by
Saint Thomas Aquinas.

Finally, I offer for your consideration a work which I
believe every American should read, <u>The Life and Selected
Writings of Thomas Jefferson</u>. More than any one of his era,
Jefferson was the chief architect of this fledgling nation.
He articulates the sense of government which we in the United
States have come to enjoy and appreciate. Harry Truman, of
whom I am a great admirer, shared Jefferson's keen ability to
blend reason and compassion in establishing a strong
government able to respond to the needs of the people. In the
1990's we can learn from both these men, that while we face
new challenges, we must temper idealism with pragmatism and
rhetoric with reason.

With best regards,

Sincerely,

George Mitchell

George J. Mitchell

MARK O. HATFIELD
OREGON

United States Senate
WASHINGTON, DC 20510–3701

March 8, 1994

Dear Mr. Kelly:

The most influential book in my life has been the Bible. My
faith guides me in every decision I make, and the Bible is a
constant source of inspiration to me.

I am also a history buff. I enjoy especially reading books on
one of my greatest heroes, Herbert Hoover. I would recommend to
you <u>Herbert Hoover Reassessed</u>, a book that disproves the
historical myth that Hoover's presidency was a "failure."

I am always pleased to hear from young people such as yourself
who take an active interest in the world around them. Please
feel free to write again if I may be of further assistance.

Kind regards.

Sincerely yours,

Mark O. Hatfield
United States Senator

Mark O. Hatfield

Politician

Senator of Oregon, Republican.

Bob Smith

Politician

Senator of New Hampshire, Republican.

BOB SMITH
NEW HAMPSHIRE

IN NEW HAMPSHIRE
1-800-922-2230

United States Senate
WASHINGTON, DC 20510-2903
November 22, 1994

COMMITTEES:
ARMED SERVICES
ENVIRONMENT AND
PUBLIC WORKS
JOINT ECONOMIC
COMMITTEE

Dear Kevin:

Thank you for your letter requesting the name of the greatest book I have ever read as well as a list of ten books I believe should be on any successful person's reading list.

What I consider to be the greatest book I have ever read is actually a series of books by Shelby Foote entitled, The Civil War.

The ten books I think are "must reads" for a well read person are:

1) The Bible (both the Old Testament and New Testament)

2) The Federalist Papers

3) Plato's Republic

4) Moby Dick by Herman Melville

5) The Civil War a series by Shelby Foote

6) The Story of Civilization by Will and Ariel Durant

7) White Fang by Jack London

8) The Book of Virtues by Bill Bennett

9) Walden by Henry David Thoreau

10) The Complete Works of Shakespeare

Best of luck to you with your upcoming book.

With warm regards,

Bob Smith, U.S.S.

CWC

DIRKSEN BUILDING
SUITE 332
WASHINGTON, DC 20510-2903
(202) 224-2841

THE GATEWAY BUILDING
50 PHILLIPPE COTE ST.
MANCHESTER, NH 03101
(603) 634-5000

46 S. MAIN STREET
CONCORD, NH 03301
(603) 228-0453

ONE HARBOUR PLACE
SUITE 435
PORTSMOUTH, NH 03801
(603) 433-1667

136 PLEASANT STREET
BERLIN, NH 03570
(603) 752-2600

PRINTED ON RECYCLED PAPER

Jesse Helms

Politician

Senator of North Carolina, Republican.

JESSE HELMS
NORTH CAROLINA

United States Senate
WASHINGTON, DC 20510–3301

February 12, 1994

Dear Mr. Kelly:

Many thanks for your letter requesting a list of the books that I've most enjoyed. How about these five?

1. The Holy Bible.

2. How Should We Then Live?, by Dr. Francis A. Schaeffer, now deceased but one of the most remarkable men I ever met.

3. The Last Lion, by William Manchester.

4. CHURCHILL, Speaker of the Century, by James C. Humes. (Yep, I've always been fascinated by Churchill -- and Jamie's book is delightful.)

5. A Turtle on a Fencepost, by Allan C. Emery. Dr. Emery offers some realistic and uncomplicated suggestions about how to live constructively and happily.

Hope this helps you in your endeavor. Best of luck and kindest regards.

Sincerely,

Jesse Helms

JESSE HELMS:wp

J. ROBERT KERREY
NEBRASKA

United States Senate
WASHINGTON, DC 20510

January 25, 1994

Dear Mr. Kelly:

Thank you for your letter. I am honored that you have chosen to include my choices in your book.

I am an avid reader, and therefore your question is very difficult for me to answer -- there are so many good books. However, for the sake of this survey, I have limited myself to just ten. The following are books that I feel everyone should try to read, but are not in any specific order:

1. Tess of the D'Urbervilles by Thomas Hardy
2. Anna Karenina by Leo Tolstoy
3. Crime and Punishment by Fyodor Dostoevsky
4. My Antonia by Willa Cather
5. For Whom the Bell Tolls by Ernest Hemingway
6. The Great Gatsby by F. Scott Fitzgerald
7. The Catcher in the Rye by J.D. Salinger
8. The Adventures of Huckleberry Finn by Mark Twain
9. Their Eyes Were Watching God by Zora Neale Hurston
10. The Sound and the Fury by William Faulkner

As for my favorite book, it is undoubtedly the Bible. There is no other book like it, and no other book that has impacted my life, and the lives of so many others, as this book has.

Once again, thank you for your letter. I hope that my response will help you in your endeavor.

Sincerely,

J. Robert Kerrey

J. Robert Kerrey

Politician

Senator of Nebraska, Democrat.

July 7, 1994

Dear Kevin:

Thank you for your letter regarding my reading habits.

I am a firm believer in the discipline of reading. I try to devote at least two hours each day to reading. I also believe that the American people have become totally dependent on the electronic media for their external knowledge. This is an expanding and tragic situation. I do not even have a television set in my Washington residence.

My reading consists mostly of non-fiction and includes newspapers, business and political magazines and current books. My secondary reading includes historical events, and the rise and fall of various governments. The events leading to World War II and the war itself are topics of special interest.

It would be difficult for me to single out one book as my favorite, but the one that stands out the most is "Treasure Island." I have read it many times and it is truly inspiring.

I hope this information is helpful. I am responding with the hope that your papers will help convince the youth of our country to dedicate more time to reading.

Sincerely,

Lauch Faircloth
United States Senator

Lauch Faircloth

Politician

Senator of North Carolina, Republican.

Arlen Specter

Politician

Senator of Pennsylvania, Republican.
Candidate for the 1996 Presidential Election.

ARLEN SPECTER
PENNSYLVANIA

COMMITTEES:
JUDICIARY
APPROPRIATIONS
VETERANS' AFFAIRS
INTELLIGENCE

United States Senate
WASHINGTON, DC 20510-3802

March 21, 1991

Dear Mr. Kelly:

Thank You for your recent letter to my office in reference to a request for the book which has most influenced my life. I have enclosed a copy of our U.S. Constitution which I feel is one of the most important documents in existence today for every American. There is no doubt that it has defintely played a very important role in my life. I hope that this will satisfy your request satisfactorily.

Best of luck to you in all of your future endeavors.

Sincerely,

Arlen Specter

AS/eb

Phil Gramm

Politician

Senator of Texas, Republican.
Candidate for the 1996 Presidential Election.

PHIL GRAMM
TEXAS

United States Senate
WASHINGTON, D. C. 20510-4302

January 11, 1994

Dear Mr. Kelly:

Thank you for your recent letter regarding my favorite book. You may be interested to know that Friedrich Hayek's classic book The Road to Serfdom is perhaps my favorite book.

The Road to Serfdom powerfully and convincingly illustrates the inevitable consequences of significant government involvement in the economy and the lives of individuals. As you know, Hayek uses an historical analysis of pre-World War II Germany's economy to illustrate the dangers of a planned economy for the citizens of any country. What may appear to be short-term benefits of centralization in reality create much deeper long-term problems which can strangle the ideas and livelihoods of a free people.

I appreciate having the opportunity to represent you in the United States Senate. Thank you for taking the time to contact me.

Yours respectfully,

PHIL GRAMM
United States Senator

PG:jpd

Orrin Hatch

Politician

Senator of Utah, Republican.

1. The Bible

2. The Republic, Plato

3. Complete Works of Shakespeare

4. Democracy in America, De Tocqueville

5. Crime and Punishment, Dostoevsky

6. Huck Finn, Twain

7. Summa Theologica, Thomas Aquinas

8. Doctor Faustus, Thomas Mann

9. Swann's Way, M. Proust

10. World War II Memories, Churchill

Edward Kennedy

Politician

Senator of Massachusetts, Democrat.

𝔈𝔡𝔴𝔞𝔯𝔡 𝔐. 𝔎𝔢𝔫𝔫𝔢𝔡𝔶
Massachusetts

United States Senate
WASHINGTON, DC 20510

April 14, 1995

Dear Kevin:

Thank you for writing to inquire about the books that have shaped me. I appreciate your interest, and I am pleased to have the chance to respond.

I would list the following books as meeting that test:

John Brown's Body, by Stephen Vincent Benet

Profiles in Courage, by John F. Kennedy

Notes of Debates in the Federal Convention of 1787, by James Madison

A Stillness at Appomattox, by Bruce Catton

The Seven Storey Mountain, by Thomas Merton

Cry the Beloved Country, by Alan Paton

Shiloh, by Shelby Foote

Thank you again for contacting me. I wish you success in your project, and I hope that it will encourage citizens of all ages to read these books and be inspired by them, as I have been.

Sincerely,

Edward M. Kennedy

BILL BRADLEY
NEW JERSEY

COMMITTEES
FINANCE
ENERGY AND
NATURAL RESOURCES
SPECIAL COMMITTEE ON
AGING

United States Senate
WASHINGTON, DC 20510–3001

March 3, 1994

Dear Mr. Kelly:

Thank you for sending me a letter inviting me to submit a reading list. I appreciate your taking the time to inquire about my taste in books.

It would be difficult for me to pinpoint the greatest book I have ever read. The following, however, is a list of a few books that have influenced my thinking about the American political process:

> *The American Political Tradition* by Richard Hofstadter
> *The Papers of Woodrow Wilson*, edited by Arthur Link
> *The History of the United States, 1801-1809* by Henry Adams
> *The Liberal Tradition in America* by Louis Hartz

I hope that this will be of assistance.

Best wishes to you and your book.

Sincerely,

Bill Bradley
United States Senator

BB/sk

Bill Bradley

Politician

Senator of New Jersey, Democrat.

```
        SENATOR CAROL MOSELEY-BRAUN (D-IL)
           TOP BOOKS PEOPLE SHOULD READ

    1. Bible (the greatest)
    2. Koran
    3. Collected Works of Shakespeare
    4. Maya Angelou (all her works)
```

Carol Moseley-Braun

Politician

Senator of Illinois, Democrat.

"Reading all the good books is like a conversation with the finest [people] of past centuries."

René Descartes, *Discourse on Method*

HISTORICAL
FIGURES

I began this portion of my book with the idea that I could best round out this work with reading preferences of influential people in history. I decided that the bulk of my information should appear in the same form as the rest of the book. So I fashioned a letter not unlike the original letter that I used to get the others to respond, and sent out to every Presidential Library, historical center, or birthplace I could get my hands on.

It took several variations to get the right letter to the right people, but the end result was quite fruitful. I believe a good mix of people is represented here. I begin with former Presidents of the United States, from Thomas Jefferson the third President to a personal letter from former President George Bush, our forty-first President (in chapter 6 of this book). The latter portion of this section concentrates on great thinkers and writers of the past.

Again, the lists come in many shapes and forms. From some people I acquired just a quote about reading, whereas for others I received complete lists with remarks backing up the selections.

Margaret Doody, author of *Jane Austen's Reading*, sums up my belief in regards to the following reading lists. "The record of what any individual has read is almost always incomplete." Undoubtedly other books shaped these individuals, but most of these people are no longer around to substantiate their preferences. We must then accept what little information we have; information derived from personal letters that mentioned and commented on books, and from libraries that the individuals left behind.

However incomplete these lists may be, I still believe that they serve as a glimpse into the reading tastes of well-known historical figures. One recuring remark mentioned to me when I collected this information was that the individual was less than successful while living. It is their success or popularity now, however, that makes knowledge of what books shaped them so important.

I am indebted to all of the people who took time out of the day to gather the necessary information for me. Credits for the people and books that provided this information may be found on pages 225 to 227. Without their help I would have been utterly lost.

Thomas Jefferson

1. *Observations on Gardening* by Thomas Payne; 2. *The Iliad* by Alexander Pope; 3. *Virgil* by John Dryden; 4. The works of John Milton; 5. *Tasso* by Hoole; 6. *Ossian with Hugh Blair's Criticism*; 7. *Telemachus* by Robert Dodsley; 8. Capell's Shakespeare; 9. The works of Henry Fielding; 10. The works of Samuel Richardson.

Andrew Jackson

"Jackson was not a book reader. His preferred reading material was newspapers. Visitors to the White House commented on towering stacks of newspapers littering every horizontal surface. He recommended to his nephew Andrew Jackson Donelson the book *Lives of the Scottish Chiefs*. He also recommended William Wallace as a role model with the assumption he must have read his works."

Martin Van Buren

As an adult he enjoyed reading books by Sir Walter Scott and James Fenimore Cooper. His collection of books was large and the number of works on all political subjects is immense.

James Polk

1. *New American Gardener* by Thomas Fessen; 2. *Patapsco and Other Poems* by Charles Soran; 3. *Pictorial Life of Andrew Jackson* by John Frost; 4. Poetical works of Sir Walter Scott; 5. *Rise and Progress of Religion in the Soul* by Philip Doddridge.

James Buchanan

1. *Almanach de Gotha 1858*; 2. *The American Reader* by Asa Lyman; 3. *Debitor and Creditor* by Timothy Shay Arthur; 4. Geometry Textbooks; 5.Holy Bible (Buchanan Family); 6. *History, Conditions and Prospects of the Indian Tribes of the United States*; 7. *The History of Rasselas, Prince of Abyssinia* by Samuel Johnson; 8. *New York Journal of Commerce*; 9. *Pennsylvania State Reports*; 10.Shakespeare (Vols. 1-8).

Abraham Lincoln

"Mr. Lincoln's interests ran nearly the whole gamut of literature. Besides text-books, reference books, occupational studies, and prose and poetic literature, we know of his having read works of history, biography, science, philosophy, law, humor, religion, government and politics."

Rutherford B. Hayes

1. *David Copperfield* by Charles Dickens;
2. Works of Ralph Waldo Emerson;
3. Works of Edward Bulwer;
4. Works of Thomas Macaulay;
5. Works of Aaron Bancroft;
6. Works of Benjamin Prescott;
7. Works of Henry Longfellow;
8. Works of John Milton;
9. Works of Mark Twain;
10. Works of Homer.

Theodore Roosevelt

1. The Bible; 2. Works of William Shakespeare; 3. *Faerie Queene* by Edmund Spenser; 4. Works of Christopher Marlowe; 5. Works of Alfred Mahan;   6. Thomas Macaulay—History, essays, poems; 7. *The Iliad and Odyssey* by Homer; 8. Selected poems by Percy Bysshe Shelley 9. Selected essays by Francis Bacon; 10. James Russell Lowell—Literary Essays, *Biglow Papers.*

Calvin Coolidge

1. Speeches of Lord Erskine of Webster;
2. Essays of Macaulay; 3. Writings of Carlyle; 4. Writings of John Fiske; 5. Translated some of the orations of Cicero (especially those attached to the defense of his friend the poet Archias, because in it he dwelt on the value and consolation of good literature); 6. Works of John Milton; 7. Works of Shakespeare; 8. Poems of Kipling; 9. Works of Field; 10. Works of Riley.

Franklin D. Roosevelt

1. Struvel-Peter; 2. *The Book of Nonsense* by Edward Lear; 3. *St. Nicholas Magazine*; 4. The Henty books; 5. Admiral Alfred Mahan's books.; 6. *A Christmas Carol* by Charles Dickens; 7. *Epitome of Universal History* by Karl Ploetz; 8. *American Birds* by Elliot Coues; 9. All of Rudyard Kipling; 10. *The Great Panjandrum Himself* by Randolph Caldecott.

Harry S. Truman

1. Read the Bible from cover to cover four to five times before he was 14; 2. *The Encyclopaedia Britannica*; 3. *Lives* by Plutarch; 4. *The Decline and Fall of the Roman Empire* by Edward Gibbon; 5. *A Child's History of England* (and the rest of his books) by Charles Dickens; 6. Works of William Thackeray; 7. Works of Victor Hugo; 8. Works of Alexandre Dumas; 9. *History of France from the Earliest Times to 1848*; 10. *Richard the Lion Hearted* and *III* and all Shakespeare's plays and poems.

Dwight Eisenhower

1. The Bible; 2. *Connecticut Yankee in King Arthur's Court* by Mark Twain because it is a wonderful satire; 3. Works of William Shakespeare because of the author's penetrating thoughts on an infinite variety of subjects; 4. Liked history (ancient and present) books; 5. Books by military leaders (volume of Napolean's diaries); 6. Reference volumes avidly; 7. Enjoyed westerns as light reading.

John F. Kennedy

1. *The Price of Union* by Herbert Agar;
2. *Oliver Cromwell* by John Buchan;
3. *Marlborough: His Life and Times* by Sir Winston Churchill; 4. *From Russia with Love* by Ian Fleming; 5. *Autobiography of Ben Franklin*; 6. *State and Revolution* by Vladimir Lenin; 7. *Wilson: The Road to the White House* by Arthur Link; 8. *The Deer Park* by Norman Mailer; 9. *The Communist Manifesto* by Karl Marx.; 10. *Decline and Fall of The Roman Empire* by Edward Gibbon.

Lyndon B. Johnson

The biographies of statesmen and leaders, particularly Andrew Jackson, Thomas Jefferson, and Sam Houston.

Richard M. Nixon

The following are books he had been reading while in the White House:
1. *The Real Abraham Lincoln* by Reinhard Henry Luthin;
2. *Tolstoy* by Henri Troyat;
3. *Mr. Wilson's War* by John Dos Passos;
4. *When the Cheering Stopped* by Gene Smith;
5. *Theodore Roosevelt* by Noel Busch.

Gerald Ford

1. Horatio Alger books; 2. The Bible; 3. Favor reading non-fiction contemporary history. As president (from the Associated Press) "President Ford read ten daily newspapers and three news magazines, and watches videotapes of television news programs."

Jimmy Carter

His favorite books are *Let Us Now Praise Famous Men* by James Agee and *War and Peace* by Leo Tolstoy. His favorite poet is Dylan Thomas.

Ronald Reagan

Favorites as a boy: 1. *Desert Gold: A Romance of the Border* by Zane Grey; 2. *Rover Boys: At Big Bear Lake* by Zane Grey; 3. *Warlord of Mars* by Edgar Rice Burroughs; 4. *That Printer of Udell's* by Harold Bell Wright. Favorites as an adult: 5. Bible (favorite book); 6. Fiction and history genres; 7. *Where I Stand* by Harold Stassen (very influential on his political thinking and positions); 8. Economic books by Milton Friedman, Friedrich Hayek, and Ludwig Van Mises as influential as well.

Jefferson Davis

1. *Spain and Andalusia* by Tenison. 2. *Court of Napoleon* by Frank Goodrich. 3. *Constantine* by Herbert Spencer. 4. *Life of Sheridan* by Thomas Moore. 5. *Memoirs* by Alexander Dumas.

Thomas Edison

1. *Les Miserables* by Victor Hugo (his daughter, Madeleine Edison Sloane, was named after one of his favorite characters out of a Victor Hugo novel). 2. *Evangeline* by Henry Longfellow. 3. The works of William Shakespeare. 4. The works of Charles Dickens. 5. *Decline and Fall of the Roman Empire* by Edward Gibbon.

Harry Houdini

"The famous exponent of stage magic has assembled the largest library of witchcraft, spiritualism and psychic phenomena to be found anywhere in the world…consisting of eight complete libraries which he has bought from time to time. More than twenty thousand books and pamphlets were purchased from Symonds, the editor of the *Banner of Light*, a spiritualistic publication of Boston."

Eugene Debs

Debs' political views had been deeply affected by these two contemporary books: *The Cooperative Commonwealth* by Laurence Gronlund and. *Looking Backward 2000-1887* by Edward Bellamy (his favorite author).

Arthur Miller

"A book that changed my life was the *Brothers Karamazov*, which I picked up, I don't know how or why, and all at once believed I was born to be a writer."

Sinclair Lewis

"When I was a boy, in the prairies of Minnesota, there was no book which had for me a more peculiar and literal enchantment than *Walden* of Thoreau."

Other authors from his father's library he read were Sir Walter Scott, Charles Dickens, Johann Goethe and certainly a volume of Milton bound together with selections from Beattie, Collins, Gray, and Young (this book Sinclair Lewis kept until his death).

Henry David Thoreau

1. *The Bhagavad Gita*; 2. *Democracy in America* by Alexis-Charles-Henri Clérel de Tocqueville; 3. Works of Ralph Waldo Emerson; 4. Works of Walt Whitman; 5. *Georgics* by Virgil; 6. *Memoirs* by Edward Gibbon; 7. *Introduction to the History of Philosophy* by Victor Cousin; 8. *Essay Concerning Human Understanding* by John Locke; 9. *The Iliad* and *Odyssey* by Homer; 10. Works of William Shakespeare.

Laura Ingalls Wilder

1. The Works of James Whitcomb Riley (including thirteen of his books); 2. *Les Miserables, Notre Dame,* and *Ninety Three* by Victor Hugo; 3. *Rung Ho* and *Tros of Samothrace* by Talbot Mundy; 4. *The Sea Wolf* by Jack London; 5. *Debits and Credits* by Rudyard Kipling; 6. *Canary Murder* Case by S.S. VanDine; 7. *Rolling Stone* by Lowell Thomas; 8. *Tales of Mystery and Imagination* by Edgar Allen Poe.

Virginia Woolf

"She highly prized *Memoirs of the Life of Sir Walter Scott* by J. G. Lockhart, a ten volume set given her by her father, Leslie Stephen. She said Scott's ordinary characters are far more interesting than his lords and ladies."

Vladimir Nabokov

"Between the ages of ten and fifteen in St. Petersburg, I must have read more fiction and poetry—English, Russian and French—than in any other five-year period of my life. I relished especially the works of H. G. Wells, Edgar Allan Poe, Robert Browning, John Keats, Gustave Flaubert, Paul Verlaine, Arthur Rimbaud, Anton Chekhov, Leo Tolstoy, and Aleksandr Blok."

Edgar Allen Poe

Poe's favorite Latin poet was Horace. He studied and liked William Shakespeare and the minor poems of John Milton.

Mark Twain

"I don't know anything about anything and never did. Personally I never care for fiction or story-books. What I like to read about are facts and statistics of any kind. With modern writers of fiction I confess I have no very extensive acquaintance. I read little but the 'heaviest' sort of literature: history, biography, travels."

Harriet Beecher Stowe

1. Read and reread Sir Walter Scott; 2. *Arabian Nights* is a volume she treasured; 3. *Magnalia* by Cotton Mather; 4. Very fond of Lord Byron; 5. Thought Nathaniel Hawthorne was the greatest writer America had.

Lewis Carroll

1. Widely read and collected Dickens; 2. Works of William Blake; 3. Works of Laurence Sterne; 4. Works of William Wordsworth; 5. Works of Christina Rossetti; 6. Works of Edgar Allen Poe; 7. Works of George MacDonald; 8. Various works on the supernatural.

Jack London

"I regard books in my library in much the same way that a sea captain regards the charts in his chart-room. It is manifestly impossible for a sea captain to carry in his head the memory of all the reefs, rocks, shoals, harbors, points, lighthouses, beacons and buoys of all the coasts of all the world; and no sea captain ever endeavors to store in his head such a mass of knowledge. What he does is to know his way about in the chartroom, and when he picks up a new coast, he takes out the proper chart and has immediate access to all information about the new coast.

"So it should be with books. Just as a sea captain must have a well-equipped chartroom, so the student and thinker must have a well-equipped library, and must know his way about that library.

"I, for one, never can have too many books; nor can my books cover too many subjects. I may never read them all, but they are always there, and I never know what strange coast I am going to pick up at any time in sailing the world of knowledge."

Ezra Pound

1. Works of Homer; 2. Works of Henry David Thoreau; 3. The Bible; 4. Works of Lord Byron; 5. Works of Dante; 6. Works of Gustave Flaubert; 7. Works of Nathaniel Hawthorne; 8. Works of Henrik Ibsen; 9. Works of William Shakespeare; 10. Works of William Wordsworth.

W. F. Cody

1. *Personal Memoirs and Observations* by General Philip H. Sheridan; 2. *Personal Recollections* by General Nelson A. Miles; 3. *Seventy Years on the Frontier* by Alexander Majors; 4. *Campaigning with Crook* by Captain Charles King; 5. *Tenting on the Plains* by Elizabeth Bacon Custer; 6. Biographies of Kit Carson; 7. Possibly some dime novels of the era.

Sir Thomas More

1. Avid reader of the Scriptures; 2. Greek philosophers (particularly Plato); 3. The Latin poets of his time; 4. Renaissance writers such as Pico and Petrarch; 5. The works of Dante.

Jane Austen

1. The Bible; 2. *The Book of Common Prayer*; 3. The works of William Shakespeare; 4. *Cecilia* by Fanny Burney; 5. *Female Quixotte* by Charlotte Lennox.

Ralph Waldo Emerson

Emerson wrote essays on the following writers: Plato, Michel de Montaigne, Johann Goethe, William Shakespeare, Emanuel Swedenborg, Plutarch. Plato and Montaigne seem to be the ones from which he learned the most.

F. Scott Fitzgerald

1. *Vanity Fair* by William Thackeray; 2. *Man and Superman* by Bernard Shaw; 3. *The Red and the Black* by Stendahl; 4. *Seven Men* by Sir Max Beerbohm; 5. *Bleak House* by Charles Dickens; 6. *Androcles and the Lion* by Bernard Shaw; 7. *Henry Esmond* by William Thackeray; 8. *A Doll's House* by Henrik Ibsen; 9. *Sister Carrie* by Theodore Dreiser; 10. *The Red Lily* by Anatole France.

Walt Whitman

"He had virtually no formal education and never went to college. What we do know is that he read everything he could lay his hands on, from Homer to the current novels and nonfiction of his day. Homer was definitely a favorite and he committed much of this to heart so that he could walk the beaches of Long Island (including Coney Island in Brooklyn) reciting aloud passages. Of course he read Ralph Waldo Emerson who influenced him greatly, but it is safe to say that he read just about everything.

Herman Melville

1. The works of Fenimore Cooper; 2. *A Visit to the South Seas* by Rev. Charles Stewart; 3. *Jane Eyre* by Charlotte Brontë; 4. *Voices of the Night* by Henry Wadsworth Longfellow; 5. Phaedo by Plato.

Robert Browning

1. Deeply fascinated by the Bible; 2. *Emblems* by Francis Quarles; 3. *Wonders of the Little World* by Nathaniel Wanley; 4. Pope's translation of Homer's *Iliad* and *Odyssey*; 5. Read widely in William Shakespeare; 6. *Paradise Lost* by John Milton; 7. Poems of Percy Shelley, Lord Byron, John Keats, William Wordsworth, and Alfred Tennyson; 8. *Robinson Crusoe* by Daniel Defoe; 9. Novels of Charles Dickens and Honoré de Balzac; 10. *Eothen* by Alexander Kinglake was his favorite travel book; 11. The plays of Euripedes and Aeschylus were favorites from the time he learned Greek at age fifteen or sixteen.

Dante

The two books that most informed Dante's imagination were Virgil's *Aeneid* and the Bible.

Elizabeth Barret Browning

1. Lover of classical literature; 2. The plays of Aeschylus, Sophocles, and Euripedes were favorites; 3. Loved the same poets as her husband; 4. Favorite novelist was George Sand; 5. Gobbled up volumes of Charles Dickens and Honoré de Balzac; 6. Valued the novels of George Elliot; 7. Also enjoyed the novels of her friend Mary Russell Mitford.

James Joyce

"If he liked a writer he tried to read everything by him. A compliment he paid to Flaubert, Dante, Ibsen, and a few others."

Benjamin Franklin

John Bunyan's *Pilgrim's Progress* was his favorite book.

Robert Louis Stevenson

"The most influential books, and the truest in their influence, are works of fiction. They do not pin the reader to a dogma, which he must afterwards discover to be inexact; they do not teach him a lesson, which he must afterwards unlearn. They repeat; they rearrange, they clarify the lessons of life; they disengage us from ourselves, they constrain us to the acquaintance of others; and they show us the web of experience, not as we can see it ourselves, but with a singular change-that monstrous, consuming ego of ours being, for the nonce, struck out."

"Books are for nothing but to inspire."

Ralph Waldo Emerson,
The American Scholar

PERSONAL
LISTS

Gwendolyn Kelly
(Grammie)

1. *Gone With the Wind* by Margaret Mitchell
2. *The Living Faith* by Lloyd Cassel Douglas
3. *The Egg and I* by Betty MacDonald
4. *Then and Now* by W. Somerset Maughham
5. *Imperial Woman* by Pearl Buck
6. *Pavillion of Women* by Pearl Buck
7. *Peony* by Pearl Buck
8. *The Houston House*
9. *The Shell Seekers* by Rosamunde Pilcher
10. *The Thorn Birds* by Colleen McCullough

Esther Goldman
(Bubby)

1. *Woman of Independent Means* by Elizabeth Hailey; 2. *Gone With the Wind* by Margaret Mitchell; 3. *Little Women* by Louisa May Alcott; 4. *To Kill a Mockingbird* by Harper Lee; 5. *Wuthering Heights* by Emily Brontë; 6. *Jane Eyre* by Charlotte Brontë; 7. *Tom Sawyer* by Mark Twain; 8. Elsie Dismore books (wanted to be as good as her); 9. *Exodus* by Leon Uris

Kevin H. Kelly

1. *Collected Short Stories and Poems* by Edgar Allen Poe 2. *Watchers* by Dean Koontz 3. *The Catcher in the Rye* by J. D. Salinger 4. *Catch-22* by Joseph Heller 5. *Metamorphosis* by Franz Kafka 6. *On the Road* by Jack Kerouac 7. *Black Elk Speaks* by John G. Neihardt 8. *Collected Poems of William Carlos Williams* 9. *Breakfast of Champions* by Kurt Vonnegut 10. *Still Life With Woodpecker* by Tom Robbins 10.5 Anything by Bill Watterson (Calvin and Hobbes).

CREDITS

- Photo on page 8 of John Landis is by Bruce Talalmon.
- Photo on page 20 of Joan Baez is by Matthew Rolston.
- Photo on page 22 of Terry Gilliam is by Julian Barton.
- Photo on page 30 of Edward Asner is by Dana Gluckerstein.
- Photo on page 32 of LeRoy Neiman is by Robert Frank.
- Photo on page 58 of Peter Bahouth is by Townsend.
- Photo on page 114 of Mary Higgins Clark is by Bernard Vical.
- Photo on page 102 of Dean Koontz is by Jerry Bauer.
- Photo on page 120 of Anne McCaffrey is by Greg Preston.
- Photo on page 158 of Michael Manley is by Marin Layacona.
- Thomas Jefferson information provided by Zanne MacDonald at Monticello.
- Andrew Jackson information provided by Sharon Macpherson at the Ladies' Hermitage Association.
- Martin Van Buren information provided by Marion F. Bernston at the Martin Van Buren National Historic Site.
- James Buchanan information provided by the James Buchanan Foundation for the preservation of Wheatland.
- Information on Abraham Lincoln found in Houser, Dr. M. L. *Lincoln's Education*. Bookman Associates, 1957.
- Rutherford B. Hayes information provided by Thomas J. Culbertson at the Rutherford B. Hayes Presidential Center.
- Theodore Roosevelt information provided by John G. Gable at the Theodore Roosevelt Association.
- Calvin Coolidge information provided by the Calvin Coolidge Presidential Center.
- Franklin D. Roosevelt information provided by Raymond Teichman at the Franklin D. Roosevelt Library.
- Harry S. Truman information provided by Benedict K. Zobrist at the Harry S. Truman Library.

- Dwight D. Eisenhower information provided by David J. Haight at the Dwight D. Eisenhower Library.
- John F. Kennedy information provided by Maura Porter at the John F. Kennedy Library.
- Lyndon Baines Johnson information provided by Allen Fisher.
- Richard Nixon information provided by Pat. G. Anderson at the National Archives at College Park.
- Gerald Ford information provided by Nancy Mirshah at the Gerald Ford Library.
- Jimmy Carter information provided by the Jimmy Carter Library.
- Ronald Reagan information provided by Diane Barrie at the Ronald Reagan Library.
- Jefferson Davis information provided by Lynda Christ.
- Information on Eugene Debs found in Ginger, Ray. *The Bending Cross: a Biography of Eugene Victor Debs.* New Brunswick, N.J.: Rutgers University Press, 1949.
- Thomas Edison information provided by Douglas G. Tarr at the Edison National Historic Site.
- Sinclair Lewis information provided by Robert Olson at the Sinclair Lewis Foundation.
- Henry David Thoreau information provided by Walter Harding at the Thoreau Society.
- Laura Ingalls Wilder information provided by Carrie A. Gray at the Laura Ingalls Wilder/Rose Wilder Lane Museum.
- Information on Harry Houdini found in Gresham, William Lindsay. *Houdini the Man Who Walked Through Walls.* New York: Henry Holt & Co. Inc., 1959.
- Viriginia Woolf information provided by Leilia Luedeking, Curator of the Modern Literary Collections at Washington State University.
- Information on Vladimir Nabokov found in Parker, Stephen Jan. *Nabokov in the Margins: The Montreux Books.* Lawrence, Kansas: University Press of Kansas, 1988.
- Edgar Allen Poe information provided by Agnes Bondurant Marcusson at the Poe Museum.
- Mark Twain information provided by Britt Gustafson at the Mark Twain House.

- Harriet Beecher Stowe information provided by Susan Zack at the Stowe-Day Foundation.
- Lewis Carroll information provided by the Lewis Carroll Society of North America.
- Information on Jack London found in Hamilton, David Mike. *Tools of My Trade: the Annotated Books in Jack London's Library.* Seattle: University of Washington Press, 1986.
- Ezra Pound information provided by Carroll F. Terrell.
- W. F. Cody information provided by Paul Fees at the Buffalo Bill Association.
- Sir Thomas More information provided by Joseph D. Crumlish.
- Jane Austen information provided by Eileen Sutherland.
- Information on F. Scott Fitzgerald found in Grapham, Sheila. *College of One.* New York: Viking Press, 1967.
- Walt Whitman information provided by Joann P. Krieg at the Walt Whitman Birthplace Association.
- Ralph Waldo Emerson information provided by Robert Makinson from the Ralph Waldo Emerson Society.
- Information on Herman Melville found in Sealts, Merton M. *Melville's Reading.* Madison: University of Wisconsin Press, 1966.
- Dante information provided by Richard Lansing at the Dante Society of America.
- Robert Browning and Elizabeth Barret Browning information provided by Richard Kennedy at the New York Browning Society, Inc.
- James Joyce information provided by Philip Lyman at the James Joyce Society.
- Information on Benjamin Franklin found in Franklin, Benjamin. *Autobiography of Benjamin Franklin.* New York: W. W. Norton & Co., Inc., 1986.
- Information for Robert Louis Stevenson found in Lee, Jasper. *Have you Read One Hundred Good Books?* 1950.

INDEX OF NAMES

228